'Camilla is an amazing, inspiring individual who has made bold, brave decisions to live the life she desires and achieve huge results. A beautiful lady whose book I know will inspire many.'
Kim Ingleby, life fitness global award-winning trainer, team GB sports therapist & NLP master practitioner

'There is a serene calmness about Camilla and I am so pleased that she has decided to write this book to share with others her approach to life.'

Lesley Joseph, actress

'Camilla has a great way of getting you to love what you are doing and just enjoy it. That kind of motivation is priceless and everyone and anyone can benefit from it.'
Mark Foster, six times World Champion & Olympic swimmer

'This book will fascinate and motivate you instantly.'
Lisa Riley, actress

D0043140

Dear Paige

May there always
be love, joy &
happiness on your
journey through life

love & light

Crista Dax

DREAM

STRICTLY INSPIRATIONAL ACTIONS

BELIEVE

FOR ACHIEVING YOUR DREAMS

SUCCEED

Camilla Sacre-Dallerup

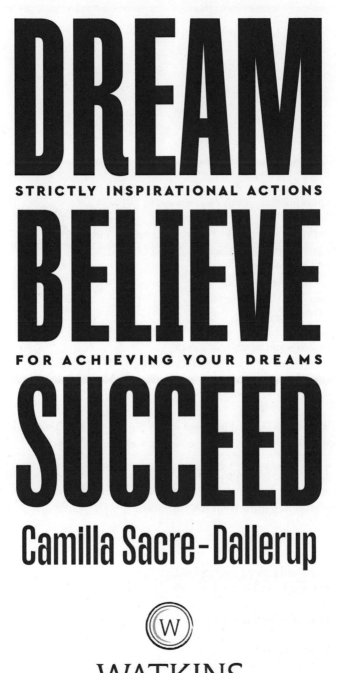

WATKINS

Sharing Wisdom Since 1893

First published as *Strictly Inspirational* in 2015

This edition first published in the UK and USA in 2020 by
Watkins, an imprint of Watkins Media Limited
Unit 11, Shepperton House
89–93 Shepperton Road
London
N1 3DF

enquiries@watkinspublishing.com

10 9 8 7 6 5 4 3 2 1

Designed and typeset by JCS Publishing Services Ltd
Printed and bound in the UK

A CIP record for this book is available from the British Library

ISBN: 978-1-78678-416-2

www.watkinspublishing.com

CONTENTS

ACKNOWLEDGEMENTS

I believe we all come into each other's lives for a reason and as I look back to the day when this book was just an idea, a dream of mine, it is with such gratitude I acknowledge the people who have helped me turn this dream into reality and ultimately share my story with you.

The biggest thank you has to go out to my Mor and Far for giving me the belief early in life that anything is possible when we work toward and believe in it; for giving me opportunities in life and letting me know that I always have a place to come home to, which has helped me feel brave and take chances in life. Thank you to my sister, Jeanet, for being a constant in my life, an intelligent sounding board and the best friend one could wish for.

And to my husband, Kevin, who believed in this project before I even started writing and when even I had my doubts that I could do it. Kevin is the most unselfish person I could have ever chosen to share my life with. His support, knowledge and ability to live fully in the now is an inspiration to me every day and I feel so grateful for the love we share.

Thank you to Maria and Dawn Slough, two wonderful ladies who helped build my brand and believed in me when the idea of a book was first discussed eight years ago. You will always have a special place in my heart and I am forever grateful for all that you have done for me to help bring me to this point. My dear friend Andrea Nash for always being there for me and always giving me an honest answer. Kim Ingleby for being my angel always.

Naomi Abeykoon, my first editor at *Bodyfit* magazine, who gave me the opportunity to share my thoughts through writing when she gave me my first column – learning to meet a deadline and creating concepts has helped spur me on to writing this book. Thank you so much for guiding me toward the right editor and publisher – I shall never forget.

Thank you to commissioning editor Jo Lal, a lady who knows her stuff and who I hit it off with immediately, your guidance has been invaluable. Thank you to my editor Karen Evennett for all your hard work. I could not have asked for a better teammate, you understood every step of the way what I wanted to achieve with my writing and ultimately the book. And to Michael Johnstone for his fantastic copy-editing and to the whole team at Watkins for believing in my dream and helping me make it happen, with all of my heart, thank you.

Lastly, thank you to three strong and inspiring women who went before me and shone the light for others to follow – Oprah Winfrey, Marianne Williamson and Louise Hay, you are my inspiration.

FOREWORD

Hi, and thank you for picking up my book. It's about living a life we enjoy, making dreams comes true, and the fact that you're about to read my story is one of *my* dreams come true. As a little girl I loved reading and having stories read to me, and I dreamed of one day writing a book of my own; but, of course, to do that, I had to have something to write about, and although I didn't know it at the time, my own life, which is based on making my dreams come true, turned out to be the perfect subject.

My first dream was to be on the stage. I wanted to dance or act, and with years of hard work – practising dance every night after school, earning my own money to help with the huge cost of training, and leaving home at 16 to improve my chances – I eventually became one of the world's top professional ballroom dancers. That dream coming true then led to my big break on the UK's *Strictly Come Dancing* (the British version of the US *Dancing with the Stars*) and a second career as a TV personality, and then a third as an actor.

Along the way I suffered every kind of hardship. I lived on next to no money, coped with a major public heartbreak, and almost had my career as a professional dancer pulled apart, but I never stopped believing that as long as I carried on working toward my goal, my dreams of success would eventually come true.

In my darkest times, I needed professional help and turned to a life coach to keep me on track – and, inspired by her and others who I met along my journey, people like Olympic gold medalist and one of my *Strictly* partners Roger Black, I am now a life coach, too. And that's fulfilling another dream – helping other people to believe in *their* dreams and take the action they need in order to succeed and make those dreams come true.

In this book, I'm going to share with you the most important lessons I've learned and some of the tools I've used – and I hope that, whatever your dream is, I can inspire you to take action toward it and more importantly find the inner happiness you deserve.

Camilla X

CHAPTER I
I SHOULD BE SO LUCKY

When people say, 'Camilla, you are so lucky!' I have to agree. I *am* lucky: extremely lucky. Lucky to have a life I love. Lucky to have travelled the world. Lucky to have met such interesting people. And above all, lucky to have achieved my dreams and found success.

Lucky? Yes! But the way I see it is that anyone can attract my kind of luck into their life when they know how. The kind of luck I'm talking about doesn't come to you like winning the lottery (even though it can feel like that when things go your way unexpectedly). The kind of luck I'm talking about had very little to do with chance. It's to do with hard, really hard, work; how carefully we listen to our instincts and act on our intuition; and how we find the bravery to step out of our comfort zone.

I would never, ever have landed my 'lucky' life if I'd just sat back and waited for fate to bring it to me. Everything I've achieved, I've worked really hard for, and along the way I've had to endure the kind of hardship that makes a lot of people give up on their dreams.

It's been a long, hard journey along a bumpy road pitted with challenges. I took the first step on that road when I was two and a half. When I finally started to reap the rewards brought by seeds planted many years before, I was 29.

That year, 2003, I really did feel as if Lady Luck was smiling on me. I'd been with Brendan for seven years: that's Brendan Cole, the dancer from New Zealand. Not only was he my dance partner, he was my soul mate and my lover. We were so close that I used to feel that I didn't know where I ended and he began. Living and dancing together, we were so much one and the same person, with one bank account, one phone and one email address.

Three years earlier, in 2000, we'd taken the huge step of turning professional after five years of dancing together as amateurs. A new millennium; a new stage in our careers. Other dancers said we were so *lucky* to have each other, 'because it can be so lonely at the top'. They were right. It can be lonely at the top and we were lucky.

The top was where we always wanted to be and we were both just as ambitious and focused as each other on getting there. And, of course, we both fervently believed we'd get to the top together.

In 2003, after making the semi-final of the Open British Championships at Blackpool, one of the highlights in the professional dancers' calendar, we were asked to audition for a new television show to be called *Strictly Come Dancing*.

We had no idea – how could we have had? – how successful *Strictly* would become, and little imagined how it would change our lives out of all recognition. But, when we heard three months after the audition, that we'd both been selected, we were dancing on air.

We'd appeared on TV before, but had never done anything like this – a prime-time Saturday night show with professional dancers teamed with celebrities. It was to run from April to June.

'Now don't you go flirting with your celeb,' Brendan joked as we jumped up and down with excitement.

I knew it was a lightly made, passing remark, but when he said it, his words did make me think that along with the fun and excitement of being part of the new show, there may be danger.

'What', I asked myself, 'had made him say it? Why had such a thought even popped into his head?'

I didn't ask him that, of course, so I'll never know the answer, but his words were to come back and haunt me a few weeks later when we were in Hong Kong for a competition. Our careers at the time were at a stage when we were dancing between 10 and 15 competitions every year. On top of that we were giving lectures, demonstrations and doing our show. Most weeks found us travelling from one country to another, from time zone to time zone. There were weeks when we'd get on a plane in London, get off in Japan and go straight from the airport to wherever we were dancing, perform, hopefully get some rest before flying on to New Zealand for another competition or maybe a show, and almost as soon as my dress had been packed, we'd be heading to the airport for a flight to China. All that in just 7 days! No wonder I spent half my life jet-lagged! That particular night in Hong Kong, we'd been travelling to one competition after another and I was absolutely shattered. All I wanted to do when we got to our hotel was put on my pyjamas, call room service, flop on our bed, switch on the television and spend the night channel-hopping. Brendan had other ideas. He was itching with excitement. 'Come on,' he said. 'Put on a nice dress and let's go and have dinner at the Hong Kong Peak Café.'

Now, during what I call 'our beans on toast years', when we'd been struggling to make ends meet as we tried to become world-class dancers, the mere idea of even walking into the Hong Kong Peak Café, never mind having dinner there, would have been almost unimaginable. The view from the restaurant is one of the most breathtaking in the world. But that was then. Now we'd turned professional, paid off our debts, bought our first home and had money in the bank. Why would I turn down the chance to eat there? So, after a bit more cajoling from Brendan and a bit of moaning and groaning from me, I ran a bath and lay in it for a time, then prettied myself up and started to look forward to having a good night out.

Brendan was being particularly attentive that night, helping me out of the taxi with a little show of gallantry and holding the door open for me when we entered the restaurant (not something he always did). When we were shown to the table he'd requested, in a romantic corner of the terrace, I realized how close I'd come to spoiling what he'd been planning to be a big night. That he'd even made the reservation was impressive as he usually left practicalities like that to me.

The way Brendan was behaving was making me feel slightly edgy and suspicious. He was excitable and kept fidgeting with his jacket and touching his pocket over and over again, the way you do when there's something in it you don't want to lose. Before I could ask him what, if anything, he kept reassuring himself was still in his pocket, a waiter arrived with a bottle of champagne. When it was poured, Brendan handed me a card with two linked hands engraved on the front. Inside were four magical words: 'Will you marry me?'

Love and hope were written across his face, and as I giggled and cried with emotion at the same time, he reached into the pocket he'd been patting all the time ... It was the most beautiful ring – a plain white gold band set with an exquisite diamond.

I was totally gobsmacked. I hadn't seen it coming at all. Brendan and I shared a bank account. How had he managed to buy a ring without me knowing?

Would I marry him? Well, of course I said yes!

Then, 'But how?' and 'When?' But what I really wanted to ask was, 'Why?'

'I took one of your rings to a jeweller to make sure I got the right size,' explained Brendan. 'And I withdrew money from our account bit by bit so you wouldn't notice, and got someone to keep it for me, until I had to pay for the ring.'

But 'Why?' I kept on asking myself.

I loved Brendan with all my heart. He was the man I planned to spend the rest of my life with. I'd even imagined us having children together. But my joy at being asked to marry him was tinged with the thought that something wasn't quite right. Hadn't we always said that we didn't need to get married, that we were already as committed to each other as we needed to be? What had changed?

As I was slipping the ring onto my finger, exclaiming at its perfect fit and admiring its gorgeous diamond, I kept thinking, 'Do we really need this?' And it was then that Brendan's words – 'Now don't you go flirting with your celeb' – came to my mind. But now they seemed to carry a meaning beyond the obvious one: 'I feel like I need to hang onto you.'

Did Brendan think I might slip away from him? Was that why he was asking me to marry him now, just as our career was about to take off in a new direction? Was he scared he would lose me?

Whether Brendan had consciously or unconsciously sensed danger ahead when he'd said that, or whether it had just been my own anxiety going into overdrive, I don't know. What I do know is that I have always had a very strong sense of intuition and I now felt that there could be trouble ahead. I knew something was about to change, that for better or worse, Brendan and I were reaching a turning point.

I am, always have been, an optimistic, glass-half-full sort of girl, someone who always has to believe that any change that comes along will be a positive one. And as I sat there, uncertain and confused about Brendan's sudden proposal, I knew I wasn't doubting my own love for him, and had no reason to doubt his commitment to me, so instead of dwelling on what was a groundless worry – at face value at least – I decided to put my anxiety behind me, tell myself that excitement and anxiety can easily be confused for one another, and be happy.

Our dinner over, we went back down from the Peak hand in hand, me gazing at the ring all the time. Looking back, I remember feeling so lucky. Lucky that Brendan and I were seeing our career go from strength to strength; lucky that we could well afford to buy lovely clothes and eat in expensive restaurants; lucky that Brendan loved me enough to secure our future together by going to all that trouble to propose to me in such a romantic way.

Enjoy life's journey and not just the destination

Little did I know that a lucky turn of events with our career was to prove so unlucky for our relationship, and though I had no way of knowing it at the time, I was about to face the toughest period of my life and go through a time when I would wonder if I'd ever be happy again.

Sink or swim?

So there I was, 29 years old and in the middle of one of the happiest times of my life – and about to face some very big challenges. But, I believe that we are all sent challenges for a reason, and that each one is an opportunity to grow and change. We always have a choice: sink or swim. And I have always chosen to swim!

And here I want to break off from my story for a while, to show you how you can make the choices that alter your luck, turning bad luck into good, and what seem like hopeless struggles into opportunities.

How to swim, not sink

By telling you the story of how I have coped with some very tough experiences, especially romantic heartache, it's my hope that my book will inspire you to listen to your own intuition and encourage you to work hard to follow your dreams. I promise you that I am 100 per cent sincere when I say that if I inspire you to make *your* dreams come true, then that's one of *my* dreams come true.

One of my mottos is, 'Enjoy life's journey and not just the destination.' I like to look at life as an adventure, as exciting or dull as we choose to make it. I believe that it's important never to look at our current situation as our final destination or a place we can't leave. Instead, I suggest that each place we arrive at in our lives and careers is simply somewhere to stop for a while, a spot we have reached that is to be explored, to learn lessons from and to help us grow as people. Then, when we are ready, we can move on to the next exciting stop.

It's a great way to envisage your life, and if you can do it, you'll never have to feel stuck or bogged down again. No matter how badly things seem to be going, they can usually get better when we change the way we perceive them. This is something I've known deep down since I was very young. Even in my teens, I remember paraphrasing a Chinese proverb to a friend who was sad and down in the dumps. 'We can't prevent the birds of sorrow flying over our heads,' I told her. 'But we can stop them making nests in our hair.' That's how I lived my life and it's a message I will continue to pass on.

Since 2010, I've worked as a professional life coach and hypnotherapist – helping clients to move on from difficult stages in their lives is something I do every day. I like to encourage anyone who feels that they are stuck in a situation to remember my analogy about life being an adventure and a journey. We may not like every place that we explore along the way, but each one gives us the opportunity to learn a little more about ourselves, for the places we dislike can, in their own way, be just as rewarding as the ones we like. Exploring these places, especially if it means going through some difficult times, does take courage. I know that, believe me.

There have been moments in my life when I've had to dig very deep to find the courage to get through the toughest of times. As well as looking to my own resources (and we all have our own resources) I've been inspired by the writings of many 'self-help' experts, whose principles I have put to the test. They include Louise Hay, Gabrielle Bernstein, Tony Robbins, Marianne Williamson, Paul McKenna, Doreen Virtue, Paulo Coehlo, Deepak Chopra. They have all helped me to find my own path to happiness and inner contentment. So when people say to me, 'Camilla, you are so lucky,' I agree, for I am so lucky to feel an inner calm that not so long ago I thought was completely unobtainable.

Dream! Believe! Succeed!

My desire to explore life began with dreaming. When I was a child I used to watch famous dancers, actors and singers on stage and television and think, 'That's what I'm going to do one day.' And I never for a moment doubted that my dream would come true.

When I did my first arena tour and performed at London's 02 Centre and Wembley, I thought of how I used to watch Michael Jackson – who was one of my biggest inspirations as a performer when I was growing up – and think of how amazing it must be to perform in front of so many people … I longed to be on that stage, and now I was!

As far as I'm concerned, it doesn't matter how unrealistic or far-fetched a dream or ambition may be. I am quite convinced that we all have it in us to achieve nearly everything we set our mind to. When I look at these words, I'm reminded of a friend of mine who had always dreamed of becoming a professional dancer, but she'd never made the leap and became a hugely successful magazine editor. 'You know,' she said to me one day, 'I really regret not sticking to dancing. I miss it so. It was my dream. But it's too late to change.'

'Who says so?' I asked. 'You, or someone who believes that you can only achieve something like that when you're young?'

She looked at me questioningly. 'Even if it is too late for you to become a performer,' I went on, 'there's another lovely way to bring dancing back into your life. You could still be a dance teacher. There are lots of fantastic teachers who started late in life. You could study for your teaching qualifications in the evening after work.'

Not long after that, that's just what she did, and she has now quit the magazine and runs her fitness/dance business. When she sent me a message to tell me what she was doing, I was so pleased that she hadn't given up on her dream when she was so close to doing so. She may not have been a dancer, but she was working in her dream world. Hers is just one story of people who have made brave choices and started new careers at a time in their lives that would have seemed impossible to others. There are many more. People like her believed that there was a way to achieve a dream, and by thinking creatively about it, they did it. You see, just like my friend, it may very well be too late to do exactly what you've dreamed about, but you can still find fulfilment doing something similar.

This book is subtitled *Strictly Inspirational Actions for Achieving Your Dreams* because I am convinced that to dream and to act and believe in your dreams are the three elements that lead to success and happiness. Having a dream and being determined to pursue it is what keeps us on the journey to achieving it even when we hit places we don't like along the way.

If you have lost track of what your dreams are, not just in work but in life itself, think back to when you were a child. A time when you believed that anything was possible. What did you dream of then? What are you most passionate about and happiest doing in your life right now? Write down your answers and look at them carefully. Ask yourself if there's a job out there somewhere that would involve doing the things that you love. You might even find a way of creating a job for yourself that involves all the things you love.

Even the biggest task becomes easier when we break it down into simple steps. Write down a couple of ideas, baby steps if you like, that would bring you even the tiniest bit closer to fulfilling your dream. Remember the old Chinese proverb: 'A journey of a thousand miles begins with a single step.' Take that first step and you are closer to reaching your goal.

Sometimes if we get too concerned about the 'how' we lose faith in the fact that it can happen. Plan and act, but keep seeing and believing that step by step the end goal will be reached.

DAYDREAM BELIEVER

So there I was, stunned by Brendan's surprise proposal and wondering why he'd sprung it on me. Surely he knew that I didn't need a ring to feel I was committed to any man, least of all him. As far as I was concerned, I couldn't have been more committed to Brendan than I already was.

At the time I couldn't begin to imagine my wedding day – but fast-forward six years to a beach in Ibiza, and there I was, in a beautiful white wedding dress, knowing that I wanted nothing more than to be married to the man standing next to me. *Hello!* magazine was taking photos and it felt just like a fairy tale come true. But the man standing next to me wasn't Brendan Cole and I knew now why it had felt so strange when he had proposed to me that night in Hong Kong. We were not really meant to end up together, after all.

When I met Kevin, the man I married, it felt like I had 'come home'. He was the Yang to my Yin, the destination-happiness I'd been journeying toward for decades. And if that sounds like a cliché, sorry, but it's true.

Best foot forward

Let's wind the clock back to the start of my long journey. It's 1976 and I'm two years old, watching my big sister Jeanet getting ready for her dance class. She's ten and as I watch her put on her dance shoes and pretty frock, I'm thinking, 'I can't wait for it to be my turn to dance.'

I was far too young for it to occur to me that I might never be able to dance, but I'm sure it had occurred to others; when I was in my Mor's womb, my left foot had folded itself up along my leg and when I was born, it had flopped out limply to the side.

Mor and Far (that's 'Mum' and 'Dad' in Danish, so that's what I call them) must have thought that maybe dancing would help to correct my poor foot and one day when I was two and a half I put on my first dancing shoes and was on my way to my first dancing class. I don't think anyone in my family ever imagined how well I would take to it. I didn't just take to it ... I LOVED IT!

Mor may have been determined to correct my foot – and I tell her now that it was her positive thinking that helped to heal it, as well as the massage she gave me every day to encourage my muscles to realign, and my dancing.

Now I tell people that I was born with a burning desire to follow my dreams, and I sincerely believe that if you say that often enough it becomes such a part of your thinking that the last thing you'll do is give up on whatever your dream is.

Because of my foot, I had to wear horrible, specially made, clumpy and ugly orthopaedic shoes. I can see now how lucky I was that my parents could afford them, for had I not worn them my foot might never have been corrected, but at the time lucky was the last thing I felt. I hated them. I made such a fuss when I had to put them on.

I also had to stand on the staircase, raising my foot onto my toes over and over again. Up and down, up and down, up and down ... it wasn't just hard, it was unbelievably boring. But it worked. All these repetitions helped build up the muscles that made my foot work properly. I didn't realize then how important repetitive exercise would be in achieving my ambition to perfect my dancing.

If I hadn't worn those shoes and done the exercises, my foot would probably still be kicking out when I walked and dancing would have been an unachievable dream. I'm telling you this now because we all have impediments, sometimes real, sometimes imaginary, that make us feel that we can't do certain things and that can put a brake on us even thinking about trying to follow our dreams. Please don't let this happen to you.

Never forget that we always have a choice. We can see a problem as an obstacle or as a challenge. See it as a challenge and it becomes an obstacle that can be overcome.

I remember my grandma sitting me down when I was eight and showing me a newspaper cutting of my Mor holding me when I was a baby. Then she told me that when I was just a few weeks old and on a family caravanning holiday, a glass lamp had cracked and fallen on my head, leaving me with what looked like a big hole in it, and covered in blood. I was rushed to hospital and Mor and the others had to wait outside while I was being stitched, not knowing if I was going to be all right. Happily, I was. Somehow, a local newspaper got hold of the story and took the photograph of Mor holding me. Grandma told me that she had been so traumatized by what had happened that she could never bring herself to tell me about it, never mind show me the newspaper cutting. The story taught me that none of us ever knows what lies around the corner, so we have to make the most of our lives while we can. Why waste even a minute?

As I said, I was eight when Grandma told me that story, and it reinforced what I already somehow knew – that if I faced a challenge I would move mountains to overcome it. I honestly can't remember a time when I didn't want to prove to the world that I could do whatever I set my mind to.

When I was growing up in Aalborg, my parents were my inspiration. Mor ran a hairdressing salon in our house and Far owned a car dealership right next door, so they were always there for my sister Jeanet and me. It was a great way to grow up. We were raised on values and beliefs that I still hold dear. *Believe in yourself. Always treat others how you want to be treated. And when you fall, get up, brush yourself off and carry on.* That last one's a bit like a line from that Jerome Kern and Dorothy Fields song Fred Astaire and Ginger Rogers sing in *Swing Time* – 'Pick yourself up, dust yourself off, start all over again!'

You shall go to the ball!

Every Christmas for the last few years, I've played the Fairy Godmother in *Cinderella*, waving my magic wand and uttering those famous words – 'You shall go to the ball.' Every time I say them brings back the sweetest memory of my own first ball when I was just three years old. Mor made me a really pretty red dress, and I remember feeling like a princess as I twirled round and round, watching the voluminous red underskirt swirl around me. Even then, at just three, dancing felt natural to me – the thing I was born to do.

It soon became so obvious that I loved dancing, that Mor enrolled me in all sorts of classes, from Latin to jazz and tap, ballet to ballroom. I also took acting and singing classes and started to think that maybe I would like to be an actress, but living in a small city there weren't that many opportunities for children to act and it would have been hard for me to get the experience I'd need if I was going to go to drama school.

But when I was six, I realized that if I competed in ballroom and Latin, then even if I couldn't be an actress, I could still be on stage somewhere in the country every Saturday. Sometimes we have to think creatively and take a roundabout route before arriving at our final destination. Now, as well as being a life coach, I have a career as an actor, but it didn't start until I was well into my 30s. And I know that the opportunity to 'tread the boards' as you say in England, would never have come along, had I not followed my career as a dancer.

And to think there was a time – a very short time – when I was five that I decided that dancing wasn't for me. It was approaching the end of the summer term and classes were coming to an end.

'Mor,' I said. 'I don't want to go back in the autumn.' I was quite adamant about it.

'Fine,' said Mor. 'I'll cancel your lessons and tell your partner he'll need to find someone new.'

Come autumn, though, and my feet were itching to dance again. I begged my poor mother to rebook my classes and try

Never forget that we always have a choice

to get my partner back. It was only years later that she confessed that she'd never cancelled my classes – she knew me too well to do that – and she certainly hadn't told my partner I was giving up: boys who danced were as rare as snow in the Sahara. Well, not quite that, but they were few and far between. Never burn your bridges: that's another lesson Mor taught me.

So there I was, back to all the hard work that got me where I am today. Lessons after school, where I was always happy with being 'good enough'. I was never academic. For me, what mattered was what happened after school. I liked to be moving about. If I wasn't dancing, I'd be playing badminton, or skating. Sitting at a desk all day made me feel as if my brain was going numb: being on my feet cleared my mind. Even now, if I have to learn lines for a speech I'm to make, or for a TV show or stage play, I do it best when I'm walking around.

As a child, whenever I was dancing I would lose myself in the movement and music. Nothing else mattered, just the connection between my mind and my body. It was like being in a meditative state – and I am so thankful that I never gave it up, and thankful to my Mor. She gave me the gentle pushes I needed, but was never a pushy mother.

I think it's also thanks to Mor that I have come to believe that no matter how old we are, playing is a great way to help us tap into our creative mind, another route to helping us find our dreams. But it's something we often give up as we grow up, like laughter, and that's really sad.

Practice makes perfect

When you're an adult, it's down to you to push yourself, and I still push myself using lessons my mother taught me when I was very young. One way she kept me on track was to question decisions I made. If I said, 'Oh, I don't really feel like practising today,' she'd say, 'Well, think about how you'll feel on Saturday if you don't do well in your competition. You'll only have yourself to blame, and you'll never know if you could have done better if you'd practised!'

Looking back I think she got the balance just right by making me take responsibility for my own decisions and choices.

In my later life, I met plenty of pushy parents when I was teaching children to dance. Often, I'd see kids who were majorly talented, but had absolutely no interest in doing well. I could see how heartbreaking this was for their parents, who were desperate for them to use their talent and succeed. But I could also see that the children were being pushed to fulfil their parents' dreams, not their own, and that was wrong. My heart went out to them, because when we follow someone else's dreams for us, even with the best will in the world, we are being untrue to ourselves. And being untrue to ourselves can be hugely detrimental to our development as well-rounded, well-adjusted people.

As a life coach, I meet a lot of people who have fallen into careers because it was expected of them. Lawyers who feel pressured into the legal profession because they come from a family of barristers or solicitors. And it's only later in life, when they've got their law degree under their belts, that they say to themselves, 'Actually, this isn't what I want to do at all. It may look like a good job, and it may pay well, but it's not my passion, and it's not making me happy.'

It's never too late to change

When you realize you are in the wrong place, it is a step in the right direction, probably the first one. We live in a materialistic world and the more materialistic we become, the more we lose track of what it is that we really want, what it is that really makes us tick, until we've become lost in a life that one day we will live to regret.

Fortunately for me, Danish culture encourages children to grow up as individuals. The system is geared toward helping youngsters to get to know themselves as people before formal education begins – the maths, the science, the Danish and, being Denmark, the English lessons. I'm so grateful for that, because sometimes the pressure to do well academically at the expense of other talents is what in the end leads to the kind of problems that make us unhappy in the career paths we decide to follow when we leave school.

If you find yourself thinking that you haven't got the life you wanted or deserved – if you are simply unhappy – then I urge you, please look at ways you can change direction. Remember the dreams you used to have and revive them. Don't live the rest of your life with regrets, they are a bar to happiness.

True happiness can only be found within yourself

Addicted to success

We can sometimes lose track of a dream when we think we've achieved it, but we don't feel any better or any happier. So we start striving for something else we think we need or want to make ourselves feel better, more valid or more important.

Success does not always mean earning lots of money, or having a top job. To some, it might mean knowing that their children have grown up into beautiful, kind, well-rounded people. To others, it might mean running 14 marathons. Or it could mean finding inner peace.

Like most people, there was a time in my life when work came first, at the expense of everything else, including my inner happiness. But now I know that *true* happiness is not something you can buy with money. It's not something that a lover or a friend can give you, or something that the best job in the world brings. Yes, they can make you feel happy, but true happiness can only be found within yourself, and comes from learning to love yourself.

Being happy and feeling good enough about yourself is the platform on which everything else is built, and anything built on it is a bonus.

You may find that hard to believe – a lot of people do when they are caught up with the traditional trappings of success, such as power or money, or power *and* money. If that's you, then hopefully, when you get to the end of this book you'll have changed your mind.

TRY THIS

Write down the word 'success' in the middle of a sheet of paper, and then draw a circle round it. Now draw lines from it, a bit like the legs of a spider, and then at the end of each one write down exactly what comes to mind – positive and/or negative – when you think about success. Don't ponder, write down what comes to mind first.

It could be anything – 'providing for my family', 'seeing my children being happy', 'being promoted at work', 'having a big house' – anything at all.

Now take a good look at your spider diagram and you may well be surprised by some of the things you have written down.

Next, think about how comfortable you are with your notions of success and then think of one word to describe how this makes you feel and write that down, too. Try and see if there are things you need to change in the future that will make this feel more comfortable to you.

Then put this aside until you get to the end of the book. Look at it again and it will be interesting to see if your priorities and definition of success have changed.

CHAPTER 3
WORK, WORK, WORK

By the time I was six, dance had become such a big part of my life that I was taking part in ballroom competitions despite the fact that legally I was too young to enter them. It was against the rules in Denmark to compete if you were under eight years old. But even though I was only six, I refused to take no for an answer. When I wanted something, I wouldn't let anything stand in my way. I live by the same motto today as then: *'Where there's a will there's a way.'*

I'd been dancing with my regular partner, Torben, since I was two and a half and he was now eight. I begged Mor to help me persuade our teacher to get us a special dispensation as Torben was eligible and needed me as his partner. We got it.

He and I continued competing together until I was nine. By then I had become so serious about dance that I wanted to train more and more and enter lots of competitions. Torben, though, didn't want to make such a commitment, so Mor found me a new partner.

Kenneth was the son of a couple my parents knew, and the two of us worked so closely over the next few years that we became like brother and sister.

We both wanted to compete in the big championships and spent several hours practising at our dance school every night as well as competing most weekends. With Torben, dancing had been for the fun of performing; with Kenneth it was much more about reaching the finals – and winning. We were so keen that we even started lessons with an international coach from the UK who came to teach us in Denmark. It wasn't long before we were excelling in the classic five ballroom and five Latin dances.

My favourite was the ballroom waltz, and because it's the foundation of most of the other ballroom dances, it was the first one we had to master. It was also the hardest. Because it's so slow, any mistakes show up easily, so Kenneth and I had to be perfectly in tune with each other to make sure we got it just right.

You lower yourself through the knees and rise onto your toes. The movement is very controlled, and unless you are in complete unison with your partner, it looks terrible, as if you are bobbing up and down like a yo-yo, completely out of sync. But once we'd got it right, it felt out of this world. Ask any dancer and they'll tell you – the waltz can overwhelm you with emotion.

Every dance we learned was completely different from the others. The foxtrot made me feel as if I was gliding across the dance floor, while the tango is much more staccato. The Viennese waltz has just a few steps, repeated over and over again – right and left turns around the outside of the dance floor in a big anticlockwise circle and then the dizzying 'Fleckeris' in the middle. The quickstep, with its skipping, 'chasséing' and hopping across the floor, is very fast and hugely energetic.

Then there were the Latin dances. The exhilarating samba; the magical rumba – known as the dance of love, it made me feel like I was creating art with my arms; the cha cha cha, with its steps similar to the rumba's but faster; the paso doble, which is based on a bullfight with the man as the matador and his partner as his cape; and the one that's the fastest of them all, the jive. Danced mostly on the balls of the feet, with countless quick flicks and kicks. I had first fallen in love with it when Torben and I had competed in the jitterbug at our dance school.

It's quite common in our sport to learn all ten competition dances when you start out, then decide to specialize in one of them when you come to know that that's where your passion lies. I found it really hard to do this, but I always had a soft spot for the rumba. It was a dance you could practise over and over again and still know that there was no limit to how much better it could get. For me, the rumba described life with its ups and downs, love and loss: without it, I don't think I could have carried on dancing as long as I did.

The year I turned 12, I spent a lot of time dreaming and wondering how it would feel to be *The underdog can do it* the Danish Latin American Dance Champions. Kenneth and I had recently made the finals, but we hadn't won. I promised myself that I would work as hard as I could so that I knew that whenever I competed I'd done everything in my power to win. When we were 15, we found ourselves the underdogs, up against previous champions. We won – and that taught me that the underdog can do it. That's a lesson that has stayed with me to this day. Not just in competitions, but in all aspects of life – even if you are not the obvious choice, you can still win a competition or get the job of your dreams if you work for it and keep on believing in yourself.

I will never forget how exciting it was hearing our names being called as the winners. The audience's applause made my heart dance with joy, and I ran onto the floor, hugging Kenneth and thinking, 'So this is what it feels like to win.'

Blackpool beckons

As a child, when everything seemed possible, along with winning the Danish Championships, another of my dreams was to go to Blackpool in the north of England. It's one of the most important places on the dance map, so you can imagine how excited I was when one of our coaches told us we were good enough to enter the Open British Junior Championships. Practically a world championship, they were held around Easter every year at the Tower Ballroom. I talked it through with my Mor and Far and told them how much I would love to go. They had a chat with Kenneth's parents. I think they all thought that it would be much too expensive, but Mor, just like me, always believed that where there's a will there's a way (maybe I inherited it from her). She would always look at a seemingly impossible situation and work out how to make it happen.

For all of us to fly to the UK was out of the question: it was far too expensive. My parents had already spent a fortune on my private lessons, dresses and shoes. But they saw it as an investment and each of my successes made all the expense worthwhile. Mor would have seen giving up on going to Blackpool at the first hurdle as a waste of the money already spent, so she came up with the idea of us all driving there. We piled into the car, drove to Esbjerg and took a ferry to Harwich. It was a 19-hour crossing – but it made the trip doable.

The ballroom in Blackpool Tower was stunning with its gold ceiling and exquisite chandeliers. But most exciting of all, it had one of the best sprung floors in the world for a dancer to perform on. As soon as I stepped onto that floor for the first time, I knew I would be back. And I have been, not once but many times, and not just for competitions – 20 years later when Ian Waite, my current professional dance partner, and I were there with our sell-out show we found posters of ourselves all over town.

That first trip to Blackpool inspired me so much, and although the town itself took some getting used to I soon grew to love it for all the fun it offered and for all its flaws, too. When we drove into town on that first visit, it was the middle of the day and even that early the streets were full of drunken hen and stag parties drawn there by the town's huge amusement park, which offers something for everyone. It was, as I'm sure you can imagine, a bit of a shock for a 12-year-old who had grown up in a quiet town in Jutland.

But our B&B, five minutes from the ballroom, was warm and welcoming, and even now when I'm in town, most recently in my first stage play, *Calendar Girls*, I still go back to the same road of B&Bs. I think it reminds me that dreams do come true.

Blackpool Tower Ballroom lit the fire in my belly that made me want to be the best I could possibly be and gave me the determination to come back as an adult and make it in the big championships.

It was also the place where I held hands with a boy for the first time. He was called Mark and it was he who, years later, introduced me to Brendan ...

There were lots of amusements in the Tower where all the young dancers hung out, and although the other children spoke different languages, for the first time I felt that I really fitted in. I was surrounded by like-minded kids from all around the world, who had travelled hundreds, even thousands of miles to be there: kids who had decided to dedicate their lives to their hobby and passion, ballroom dancing. It felt so good to be one of them.

It was a tough competition. You have to enter all five dances, as usual, but in the Blackpool Juniors they have special one-dance events, as well. Kenneth and I went in for the Viennese waltz and were thrilled when we made the final.

There were many more annual Blackpool trips with my family. When I was 15, we added another yearly competition to our schedule: the International, in London. The heats were held in Brentwood and the finals in the Albert Hall, one of the city's most iconic buildings.

We also went to Norway a couple of times a year, either for competitions or for coaching. Going on all these trips with Kenneth, his parents and my Mor and Far was such fun. There's a Danish expression, '*vi hygger os*'. It sort of means having fun together, being cosy with each other. When the six of us were somewhere for a competition, '*vi hyggede os*'.

By this time, Kenneth and I were hooked, not just on dancing, or entering competitions. We liked winning.

Have you ever wondered why, when we grow up, we often stop wishing exciting things would happen to us. When we are children we find it so easy to dream and believe that our dreams will come true. When someone asks us what we would like to be when we grow up, we just come out and say it: firefighter, nurse, actor, and we're 100 per cent sure that we'll be a firefighter, nurse or actor. We don't stop and say, 'Hang on! How exactly am I going to do it?' or, 'How will I find the money for the education?' or, 'Where will I live?' or think of any other practicalities. No! Everything is simple. As children we see a bike, we want the bike, we get the bike. Even if we don't know how to ride the bike, we believe that it's possible to ride the bike and we just keep trying until we can do it.

Later on in life, we become rather good at making assertive decisions not to do certain things. We create excuses, or 'limited beliefs' as I like to call them, to stop ourselves doing exactly what we want to do and probably what we are meant to do. The good news, though, is that since it's ourselves who have created these obstacles in our lives, it's ourselves who can undo them, too, and I have found tools that helped me to do this.

I think there is something very beautiful about the fact that when we were children, we honestly believe that anything is possible, and I think that holding on to some of that when we're adults is vital for a happy and successful life. So, with that in mind, try this exercise …

- Note ten things you dream of doing whilst on this planet.
- Write down all the reasons why you haven't done them yet, and take a good look at the reasons.
- Now throw away the list of why you didn't do them. Those reasons are just limited beliefs that are holding you back and you don't need them any more.
- Now we are going to reframe and plan for achievement. Write down the five of the ten things you dream of most, then for each of these five, write three steps you can take toward making it possible.
- Write down how it would make you feel once you have reached these dreams/goals.

How do you feel about your dreams? Excited? I hope so.

Just as important as goals that are realistic and achievable are the dreams that sometimes seem a little out there. I have had dreams that I have made a reality, but if you had asked me when I first thought of them, 'But how will you do that?' I would have told you that I had absolutely no idea … Yet I didn't let that stop me from taking steps in the right direction, and believing that somehow it would happen. The important thing is not to let hurdles stand in your way – and certainly don't be the one to put up those hurdles! A wise actor once said to me, 'If I can't find a way over something, I work out how to get around it.'

I think fondly of a friend who, in her 30s, quit a good steady career with the police to open a spa because she wanted a job that would use her spiritual talents. She didn't listen to the people who thought she was mad to leave such a secure position and take such a gamble – and six years on her business is flourishing and, most importantly, she's doing a job that she loves every day. Now you might be thinking, 'Yes but she was in her 30s. What if I'm in my 50s or 60s …?' Well even age doesn't have to stand in our way. I always take inspiration from the author Louise Hay. She started publishing her own books when she was in her 50s, and ended up building an internationally acclaimed company publishing many successful authors.

Of course, big decisions like these must be taken mindfully. You may want to consider how your actions could impact on the people close to you, especially your partner should you have one. If you are the main earner in your family, for example, certain things might need to change for you to be able to switch direction, and it might be that what feels right to you is not what's right for your partner. You may need to think outside the box to make these changes possible, for example sacrificing certain comforts – selling your car, renting out a room, or taking on a different, less satisfactory job but one with better hours that gives you more time to follow your dream.

Certain things might need to change for you to be able to switch direction

Sometimes when we make major changes we rattle the foundations of our lives – and this can cause relationships to flounder. So it's really important to be open and honest with your partner, and yourself, about what it is that you want to achieve and why. Write down the pros and cons before starting out so that you are aware of the risks that you may be taking.

CHAPTER 4

EARLY LEARNING – SEVEN LESSONS I LEARNED AS A CHILD

1. It's tough being different

As a child I loved my life, travelling to dance competitions with Kenneth, giving them my all, and winning as often as we could.

But my commitment to dancing made me different from most other children – and as every schoolchild knows, being different makes you unpopular. I was so unpopular that it soon became a place to dread. I'd started off at a lovely little school where I had friends I'd known since kindergarten. They understood that I was the girl who danced, and they didn't hold it against me. But when I was eight, we moved to another part of town and I moved school, too – and being not just the new girl, but the girl who danced, made me different from everyone else. My schoolmates viewed me with suspicion, teasing me and picking on me at every opportunity.

If I'd had the right words, maybe I could have explained to the others what I did every day in my dance classes, and maybe that would have helped them warm to me. But, when you are a child, you don't know these things. So, the more they teased and the more they left me out, the more withdrawn and defensive I became.

But I knew that when I somehow got through the school day, then my other life, the one I really cared about, at the dance school would begin. I didn't have time for after-school play dates and birthday parties, and not having the type of social life that most children take for granted was just the first of many sacrifices I would have to make in order to succeed as a dancer. As I grew a bit older, I missed out on parties and girlie sleepovers. And, when I hit my mid-teens, I would sacrifice the thing that preoccupied most of my female contemporaries, dating boys, because I literally had no time for any boy who wasn't (a) on the dance circuit and (b) my partner.

2. The female of the species is more deadly than the male

Having danced with Torben from the age of two, then Kenneth from when I was nine, I was used to male company from an early age. Alongside ice skating, dance is unique in sport in that girls and boys work so closely together, and maintain one partnership for years. Torben and (especially) Kenneth were like brothers to me, we were so close; and at school I found I also felt more comfortable chatting to the boys – they were far less complicated than the girls. I always found the bitchiness and gossiping that seemed to go hand in hand with girl friendships hard to be around. I had no time for people who liked you one day and hated you the next – it made me feel uncomfortable.

Little did I realize, though, that my hanging out with the boys would make the girls even more nasty than they often had been. It came to a head one horrible evening that remains one of my worst childhood memories. I was 12 years old and, for once, had finished dance practice early enough to go to what we called a classmates' party – one where the entire class was invited, and nobody was missed off the list. I was so excited! Even if the girls weren't my best buddies, there'd be plenty of boys I liked and could chat to.

But, when I arrived, no one spoke to me. Even boys I thought of as friends turned their backs on me. I felt as if I was invisible. It was unbearably hurtful. I simply couldn't understand what I'd done to be snubbed like that.

Then one friend, bless him for being so kind, came up to me and said, 'Camilla, some of the girls got together and asked us all not to speak to you.'

I'll never forget the jolt of shock that hit me like a bolt of lightning, and the tears that pricked my eyes before I turned and ran from the party as fast as I could.

With hindsight, now that I have worked with many clients who have suffered serious traumatic experiences, I know that this was nothing really major. But trauma is relative and to me, at the time, it was devastating. Big or small, trauma can have a major effect on us and leave an emotional scar that will need healing later in life.

Unfortunately the teasing and being made to feel like an outsider didn't only happen at school. It was happening at my dance school, too, somewhere that was usually my safe haven. Some of the girls there had decided that I didn't fit in there because they thought I sucked up to the teacher. Being eager to learn, I'd ask questions and sometimes stayed to practise after class. There was an older girl I looked up to because I thought she was a really amazing dancer. The other girls took against her, too, and decided to call her 'Sticky' and me 'Mini Sticky' because the way they saw it, we always stuck to the teacher and they didn't mind letting us know that this was what they were saying about us! I was so hurt when I found out that was how they felt about me. I wasn't sucking up to anybody. All I ever wanted to do was learn, improve on what I'd learned, and fit in.

I just remember this time of my childhood as being hideous – I felt like I didn't belong anywhere.

3. Adults get it wrong too!

As if to rub salt into my wounds, one day my dance teacher, who I adored, made a joke about my legs in front of the whole class. 'When Camilla dies,' she said, 'the stork will have the skinniest legs in the world again!'

Everyone was giggling, looking at me and repeating the joke. My face was burning, my heart was racing, and my eyes were filling up with tears. My immediate impulse was to turn and run out of the room as fast as I could, but then something told me that she hadn't really meant it nastily. I think, in a funny sort of way, she was actually trying to pay me a compliment – but it was such a backhanded one that it left me feeling wounded for years. Not just that, it made me wary of other people as you never know quite when someone's going to lash out at you with a cruel remark. I certainly hadn't been prepared for that one and felt crushed by it.

Working with clients, I've come to realize that we all have to learn to love our bodies. Those with curves often wish they didn't have them, while those without any curves would give the world to have them!

We should always think before we speak

Whatever we are teased or bullied about hurts – but we don't have to let it get us down. In the end I reached the point where I decided I wasn't going to let them make me change who I am. It wasn't easy, but reaching that conclusion was a way of reaching self-acceptance, too.

That wasn't the only thing I learned from my experiences of being teased when I was a child, I came to know that we should always think before we speak: what we may think of as a harmless, throwaway remark could hurt the person it's aimed at for years. So now if I'm ever tempted to make one, I think, 'How would I feel if someone said that to me?'

And I also learned that we always have our critics. In order to pursue a career that put me in the public eye, I would have to get used to that. Friends in the dance world and that teacher would not be the last people to call me names for being skinny – and I wouldn't be the only one to be hurt by it. Years after my teacher had joked about my legs, when I was engaged to Kevin, I went on *I'm A Celebrity ... Get Me Out Of Here!*, the TV show where various celebrities are stranded in the jungle with few creature comforts. I was struggling to cope with how hungry I was and became so dangerously ill that I had to quit the show within days. People online and even journalists in newspapers, somehow felt entitled to call me malnourished, and to imply that because I was skinny I must have an eating disorder. By that time in my life I was able to cope with the comments, but my husband-to-be, Kevin, was devastated by them.

4. Anger is toxic

Being teased as a child left me feeling angry and upset for a long time. I couldn't help asking myself over and over again what I had done to deserve this? I now know how toxic anger can be. Anger eats away at you, it changes who you are and how you act. It made me cautious and mistrustful of other people, and I went into survival mode, becoming quite cold and telling myself that the other girls were just jealous because I had a talent that made me special, and better than them. I know now that thinking in that egotistical way was doing me no favours at all. Nobody is any better than the next person, but sometimes we have to work hard to remember that.

In years to come, knowing the damage it can do, I learned to let go of anger. I also learned that we always have a choice. We can either attack someone who makes us angry, or, following the example of Gandhi and more recently Nelson Mandela, we can show the people who are trying to anger us that we love them.

5. Do unto others as you would be done by

There are two characters in Charles Kingsley's *The Water Babies* – the kindly Mrs Doasyouwouldbedoneby and the miserable Mrs Bedonebyasyoudid. Guess which one my lovely parents encouraged me to be like. 'Always treat others as you would like to be treated yourself,' they would say. So, after my nightmarish experience at that school party, I decided I would always go out of my way to make sure I never excluded anyone from a group I was part of. If I could sense that someone was struggling to join in, I would help them. I may have learnt that the harsh way, but, guess what, I now thank my classmates for teaching me that lesson.

As a life coach I have learned that we can always turn a negative situation into a positive one. You just have to look at it from a different angle, and think, 'OK, that wasn't very nice – but what can I take away from it that will help me in the future?' There is nearly always something positive to be found.

As a child, I never felt as if I really fitted in the way the others did – and I am now hypersensitive to other people who feel that way.

6. Bereavement puts everything in perspective

I was 13 when I suffered my first bereavement – the loss of our dog, Besy. She was a beautiful German Shepherd who'd slept next to my pram from the day I was born and had protected us when someone tried to burgle my Far's showroom next door to our house.

She was my best friend. Whenever I felt sad, it was Besy I'd reach for. Losing myself in a soft, doggy cuddle, and feeling her unconditional love pouring over me always made me feel much better.

I adored that dog and couldn't begin to imagine life without her, so when she suddenly became ill and my Far took her to the vet's and came home alone I was utterly devastated. One moment I was numb with disbelief, the next I was crying hysterically. I sobbed and shook all the *We all grieve in* way to Norway, where Kenneth and I *our own ways* were to dance in a competition. It was the first time I'd felt such deep sadness, and it was a pain I wasn't keen to experience again. But I also learned that as horrible as grief is, we can eventually move on. Going through it for the first time at 13 was tough, worse than tough, but it helped me cope when the same kind of loss struck me out of the blue years later when my relationship with Brendan came to a very abrupt end.

We all grieve in our own ways – sometimes grief doesn't hit until long after a loss because the immediate shock was so great, or perhaps because it is put to one side until we are psychologically ready to cope with it.

Ultimately, though, even grief can be a helpful emotion because it helps other situations to be put in perspective. When Besy died, the pain I had felt at being shunned by my classmates, being given a cruel nickname at dance school and then being called skinny by my teacher was nothing, absolutely nothing, in comparison to the pain I felt at losing Besy, and would feel again when I lost Brendan.

I remembered what I had told my friend about the birds of sorrow flying over your head, but you don't have to let them make nests in your hair. In other words, I had a choice. I could dwell on the sadness and gain nothing from it; or I could celebrate the love I'd had for Besy and be grateful for the time she and I had shared – and that was what really helped me find my way back to happiness.

7. Love is all you need

When things weren't going well in my life, I had Besy and my family to turn to. I felt loved, and I knew I was lucky to have that – not everyone does.

Sometimes we are teased or bullied by friends or family who don't necessarily share our positive outlook. When all we really want is for the people close to us to be jumping up and down with excitement, offering us words of support, they say negative things to us like, 'Do you think that's a wise idea?' or, 'Do you really think this is possible for you?' or even, 'I don't think you have what it takes to do this.'

What we must remember is that comments like those are actually due to the limited beliefs of the people who make them. We can protect ourselves from them – the negative comments not the people – with this simple exercise that I have used throughout my career.

When you've been hanging out with someone whose negativity seriously drains you and leaves you feeling not just exhausted but also in a bad mood, try to imagine the next time you have to meet up with Mr or Ms Negativity, that there's a bubble around you and their attitude will simply bounce off it. The bubble can have more than one layer and can be of different colours. Maybe a red one will send the negativity packing, a blue one will attract any negative feelings you may have and see them on their way, and a green one will let positive energy through to you. The colours don't matter. I'm sure you get the idea. You can also imagine a bubble around the other person that keeps their negativity in. I call this my protective bubble exercise. It works for me. I know it will work for you.

Choosing your words carefully will help you create your protective bubble. If someone else uses attack words such as, 'I don't think that's your sort of thing,' or, 'You're never going to achieve it,' the last thing to do is to retaliate. Instead, stay calm and say something positive. 'I'm really excited about it!' or maybe, 'Taking on this challenge seems right to me,' or even better, 'I would really love your support but quite understand if you can't give it to me right now.' Remember they don't know what you are capable of, only you do; and starting a tit-for-tat slanging match will resolve nothing. As long as you know within yourself that it doesn't matter to you whether or not they believe you can go where you're going: you know you can. And will.

I am sharing exercises like this because I wish I'd had them up my sleeve when I was at school – but I didn't. I did however use them later on in my competitive career, and still do today in my new life.

UNDERSTANDING YOUR INNER CHILD ...

As an adult, have you ever been in a situation where you think, 'OMG, this is just like being 6 or 8 or 15 again'? I learnt to deal with times when I felt excluded and other unpleasant moments when I realized that nobody else can make you feel a specific way. You and only you are responsible for how you feel. When I was younger, if someone hadn't invited me to a party or lunch or whatever I would have been upset. Now, I feel good enough in myself that I don't actually care about such trivial things because I'm totally OK with me. That's not to say that I don't like being invited by friends to go somewhere and have a good time with them, but it's great to find the kind of inner peace that means my happiness doesn't depend on whether or not I get that invitation. Yours doesn't either.

I've studied the principles of NLP (Neurolinguistic programming) and other therapies, and thanks to them have come to believe that events from our early lives can determine how we react in certain situations in our adult lives if the issues these events have thrown up have not been dealt with. Say, for example, that you were bullied at school or found yourself in any other situation that made you feel unloved, lonely or even abandoned. This would have made you feel very isolated and perhaps, deep down, that you were not a good enough child. Wind the clock forward. You're a grown-up and you find yourself in a situation maybe at work, maybe at home, where people seem to be putting you down. Instead of standing up for yourself as an adult should, you are brought right back to that time at school and you revert to the same childish behaviour – with tantrums, outrage and probably words you later have to apologize for. Perhaps you recognize this behaviour in yourself – later asking yourself, 'Why? Why didn't I just ask, "Do we have a problem here?"' or, "Is there an issue we need to resolve or talk about?"' Why, you wonder, didn't you deal with the situation in a grown-up way?

Let me tell you why. You didn't react in an adult way because you haven't dealt with and let go of that old childhood behaviour. It could have been created at school or at home by your relationships with your sisters, brothers or parents. It could be that someone you loved dearly had no time for you, or someone whose attention you craved ignored you, maybe you were hurt and angered by being bullied. Perhaps someone you loved died, or moved away. Any of these things can result in our feeling that deep down we don't feel good about ourselves.

TRY THIS ...

Wherever, whenever and whatever it was that created that sense of inadequacy, learn to accept that it was *then* and not *now*. 'Now' is different, and you have a new opportunity to deal with things in a new way. If you now notice the challenge that has been sent your way, you can use it as an opportunity to create a new pattern right away. Remember, this time around, you are good enough. Remember that you love yourself! If you don't fully love yourself yet, it's probably about time you did! Remember, if you truly feel good enough inside to the point you can look yourself in the mirror and say, 'Hey you, I love you. You are fabulous!' then no one can ever make you feel any differently because you know that you are good enough and that's all that matters! I have been hugely inspired by Louise Hay and all her wonderful books. She often talks about mirror work: actually speaking to ourselves in the mirror and saying nice things. It may sound slightly out there to some of you, but if you are not going to say nice things to yourselves why should anybody else? I see it as a great place to start! The first time you do it, of course you feel more than a little self-conscious. That feeling soon goes. Promise.

HERE'S SOMETHING ELSE TO TRY

Take a piece of paper and write, 'Why I'm good enough' at the top of the page. Then write down ten reasons why you are good enough and why you should love yourself now. For example, 'I'm a great friend, mother, lover or daughter,' or even, 'I am smiley, I spread happiness wherever I go' … 'I'm funny!' … You get the idea.

And next time you look at yourself in the mirror say, 'Hey Lovely (or Handsome), you are totally good enough. In fact, you are not just good enough, you are awesome.' You may not believe it the first couple of times, but after a while you will. It's also a great thing to say to your closest friends. Not that you are awesome, but that they are. I often tell my friends that they look fantastic and that I think they totally rock. Love spreads love, so start by loving yourself.

NOW TRY THIS …

Think about the situations in your life, at home or at work, which you have reacted to in an undesired manner and write them down. Then try to see if you can identify a pattern, and now you are aware of it, try to work out when it was created. Note the past tense – 'created'. It's in the past. You can let go of it now. You no longer need to react the way you have been. Consider a new way to behave when you are in a similar situation from now on.

CHAPTER 5
MONEY, MONEY, MONEY

Training, travelling, dresses and shoes – they all add up to make dancing an expensive sport. And the more Kenneth and I progressed, the more anxious I became about the fact that most of my parents' spare money was going on me and my dancing.

At 12 years old, I hit upon a way of helping them by starting a little business of my own – buying tracksuits from my grandad, who had a finger in lots of pies, and selling them. He could do many things, but he couldn't model ladies' tracksuits. I could though, and that's what I did – to Mor's clients when they were having their hair done at her salon.

The tracksuits were bright and colourful, and made of cotton, stylish enough to go with jeans. I realized quite quickly that whenever I wore one myself in Mor's salon, the customers would say, 'That's nice.' So when they did I'd tell them that I was selling them and asked if they would like to buy one. And that's how I understood that after *Strictly*, brands like Aristoc tights and Ariella couture asked me to endorse their range by being seen wearing them!

At around the same time that I was selling the tracksuits, I used to love playing at being interviewed on British television about my career. And guess what I was doing after I joined

Strictly? Giving interviews to British television about my career. How could I have known that when I was standing in the bathroom, holding a shampoo bottle and pretending it was a microphone, I was visualizing and sowing seeds for the future?

When I was 14, I upped my game and joined a modelling agency that sometimes paid me in clothes: one less expense for my parents. Sometimes I'd rope in Kenneth to model with me and we'd put the money we earned toward our training. We needed every penny we could get because we wanted to train with one of the best coaches on the circuit – a Norwegian dance champion called Tor Floysvik.

Strictly the best

Tor had a reputation for thinking outside the box, and getting his students to do the same thing. Before I met him, I'd never heard of *visualization* – creating powerful mental images that would improve the way we performed. But when he was training us, if I was struggling with a step, he'd say, 'Sit down, close your eyes, and imagine yourself doing that step perfectly over and over again.' Once I'd done that, I'd stand up, and believe that I'd done it better! And next time I did the step, I did do it better. I find it extraordinary how the mind apparently doesn't know if you are actually doing something or just imagining it. This is how powerful visualization can be, and I now use it all the time.

To train with Tor, we had to travel to Oslo by boat – yet another expense – so I persuaded one of the ferry companies to sponsor us. In return for free travel we promised to dance for them at travel fairs, and to wear their logos on our tracksuits. It was a win, win, win situation, getting us extra exposure, and also the satisfaction that the company thought highly enough of our dancing to have us represent them publicly.

We travelled to Oslo as often as we could to train with Tor, usually during the school holidays when we had time to be away from home for several days in a row, staying in one of the bedrooms attached to the dance studio. Kenneth and I had known each other for long enough for us to think of ourselves as brother and sister, so even when we were 15 years old we could share a room without being embarrassed by anything. When you spend as much time together as he and I did you come to know each other inside out. I had no qualms about telling him if his feet smelt or if he had bad breath. And he was just as upfront with me. When you dance closely with someone, you can't escape things like that.

Tor was tough, really tough, to train with. He woke us up at 7am and sent us on early-morning runs. And then we'd spend hour after countless hour on our dancing. But he really opened up our minds and I'd never felt as ready for a competition as I did after being trained by him.

He taught us that, just as with all things in life, some things were in our control, and others never would be. Our dancing, our stamina and our state of mind were things we *could* control. But the music we had to dance to, the quality of the dance floor, the judges and the other competitors were not. Like them or not, we had to put up with them.

'Just focus on those things you can control,' he'd say. 'And try not to worry about the rest.' Words that have become a mantra for me and words I love to share with my clients.

And talking of mantras, at 16 and keen to fund my training as much as I could and not just rely on my parents, I got myself a job at the first high-tech gym to open in Aalborg. I'd been asked to model for their brochure and during the shoot, I seized the opportunity to ask if they needed any staff – and landed a part-time receptionist job that fitted perfectly around all my dancing. If you don't ask, you don't get, and that's another of my mantras. When I'm with my life-coaching clients I often ask them: 'How has NOT asking worked out for you so far?' And that's something that really makes them think.

Just focus on those things you can control

41

Dilemma

I enjoyed earning my own money, and showing my parents, who were investing so much into my sport, that I was genuinely dedicated to dance, but I had a dilemma: I loved modelling, too.

I'd started it as a way of funding my dancing, but it had led to a couple of jobs in TV commercials – an exhilarating introduction to acting – and now I was starting to wonder if perhaps I was meant to put the dancing on hold and go down a different route. Even at 16, I was getting strong signals from my intuition – something I often have to teach clients to tap into – so, to see if I really was meant to change direction, I entered a magazine competition to win a contract with a US acting agency.

I wanted that fantastic prize more than anything else in the world. I'd always watched lots of American and British TV, and longed to live in an English-speaking country. This was my big chance to act, or could have been. When I heard that I'd made it to the final, it looked as if my life really could be about to change. My heart was racing with excitement, and then I read further down the letter and realised, to my horror, that the final of the competition clashed with one of the biggest championships on the dance calendar – the Danish 10. Kenneth and I had spent months preparing and perfecting our waltz, tango, foxtrot, Viennese waltz, quickstep, cha cha cha, samba, rumba, paso doble and jive. All that time and money spent on training with Tor was for competitions like this one. I couldn't back out now! I had to choose the dance competition, and, when we took the silver trophy, I knew I'd done the right thing.

I could have gone to the magazine final for the contract with an American acting agency, and maybe won or come away with nothing, but, for years, I couldn't help wondering what would have happened if I had gone and won. We all have regrets about things we think we've missed out on, but, as my Mor always used to say, 'What's meant for you won't pass you by.' In other words, if something is meant to be, it will eventually happen – when the time is right.

Find your path

Here was the real problem. I had more than one dream and thought that meant having to choose one over the other. I wanted to be a world-class dancer, but I also wanted to act. I now know that they are not mutually exclusive. Just because you follow one dream doesn't mean you have to say goodbye to the others. Giving up on an ambition is like being on the road to regret. I never gave up on my acting dream, and I did eventually go on to become an actor many years later. What was meant for me didn't pass me by.

As I grew up I learned that we can nurture and fulfil more than one dream. So, however many dreams you have for yourself, hang on to them and grab every opportunity that will help you to make them come true. You may be destined to have a multi-career life like mine.

TRY THIS ...

Make yourself what I call a display dream board – other people call it a vision board – using pictures from magazines, brochures or newspapers that inspire and enhance your dream. These could be pictures of a place you would like to visit, or the kind of house you would like to live in one day. Or, if you're looking to bring romance into your life, you may choose pictures that make you think of love.

It is important to write down the main emotion that your pictures evoke in you: will you feel happy, relaxed, contented or secure when these things in the pictures come into your life? You can make your dream even more tangible by being specific and putting dates by your goals. Hang your dream board somewhere where you'll see it every day, and, when you look at it, notice the wonderful feelings you experience when you imagine those dreams coming true. This is what visualization is all about.

CHAPTER 6
SWEET SIXTEEN

Once they hit their teenage years, all dancers who are serious about their sport have to spend so many hours every day with their partner that there's rarely time for what preoccupies most teenagers. Dating! And at 16, I was about to learn that couples who are together on stage are together off stage, too.

Kenneth and I had been dancing with one another since we were nine. We loved each other like brother and sister (well, like brothers and sisters who get on) and I couldn't imagine partnering anyone else. Our school days were coming to an end, so it was the time for decisions. We were both going to go to further education colleges, but would it be one that led to a practical qualification or one that would be a precursor to going to university? I hadn't really given the matter much thought, but the decisions we made would impact the time we had to dance. And so, when Kenneth chose the academic one, we both realized his dancing career was going to have to go on the back burner.

Parting with him was my first experience of a break-up – I was losing one of the closest people in my life, and it hurt. But even so, I wasn't about to give up on my dream. I still wanted to dance, that's why I decided to go to business school and study for a qualification to fall back on.

My coaches looked around and came up with a new dance partner for me – Klavs. I know it sounds like a cliché, but he really was tall, dark and handsome. He had lovely curly hair and the kindest hazel-brown eyes. There was just one snag, though: Klavs lived in Copenhagen, a four-and-a-half-hour journey by road and sea from my home in Jutland.

The only way we could train together was if we lived close to one another. Aalborg is a lovely little city, but compared to Copenhagen, Denmark's wonderful capital, there was little it could offer Klavs. Copenhagen had better trainers, better training facilities, and better transport links to the UK, where many of the important dance competitions are held. It was a no-brainer, so I packed my bags and headed for the big city. I moved into the beautiful penthouse that Klavs' family owned and took an after-school job in the bakery that they ran.

Klavs was better at ballroom than Latin, and, although I was Junior Latin Dance Champion, my long-limbed body was actually better suited to ballroom, so we focused on that. And we did brilliantly! If we didn't come first in the competitions we entered, we were almost never out of the top three.

We won the Italian and German Open Youth competitions, making it to the top 48 amateur dancers in the world at just 16 and performing in London's Royal Albert Hall. I was now so serious about my dancing that when we came fourth in the Danish Championship it felt like taking a booby prize. When I got home that night I picked up my diary and scrawled, 'Fourth place – Bad Mood!'

Looking back, in the grand scheme of things it wasn't really such a big deal, but back then it was huge. Being fourth meant we lost our funding, which only went to the top three couples. Without it, our dancing careers didn't progress as fast as they would have had we been even only one place higher.

First love

Living in the same apartment and dancing together every day could never have worked unless Klavs and I hit it off. And we did: we hit it off so much that, after a first kiss, an oh-so-precious first kiss, we found ourselves falling in love.

I couldn't have picked a more suitable boy to fall in love with, for Klavs shared my beliefs and values. I'm sure that if I'd met him later in life, we could have made a serious go of it. But sometimes we meet the right person at the wrong time, and, sadly, although it took me a couple of years to realize the fact, it was the wrong time for us.

My life was a whirlwind of business school followed by working in the bakery and then training every night. Fortunately, I'd read about a Danish businessman who power-napped in his office chair, holding his keys in his hand. When they dropped, the sound woke him and he knew it was time to get back to work. If power naps work for him, I thought, maybe they'll work for me with my schedule that was so tight that I couldn't risk oversleeping and missing work or training. So 20 minutes every afternoon found me asleep in a chair, and when I woke up I was raring to go.

Dancing's dark side

After two years of living like that I was physically and mentally exhausted. I'd been ill with pneumonia and forced to spend a few weeks at home to recover. I'd also started to see another side to the dance world, and it was a side I didn't like. The same people who coached us were also in the pool of experts from whom the judges at dance competitions were drawn. In some events, there could be two out of the seven judges who knew me well. In others, it could be just one, or even none at all.

By the time I was 18 I'd come to the conclusion that it was impossible for the judges to be truly impartial. If they knew a couple, then that was bound to influence how they marked them. And that wasn't fair. Unless a couple are head and shoulders above the others, then it must be impossible for there to be a clear winner. In football, the team who scores the most goals wins the game. There's no goal line in my sport. It's not just about glamour, glitter and perfectly synchronized movements: it's about, or should be about, what's fair and what's not. And once I'd started to think that the competitions and the method of judging were unfair, I couldn't shift that idea. I came to believe that the system would work much better if coaches only coached and judges only judged!

For the first time in my life I started to seriously question whether I really wanted the life of a dancer. Not only did I become completely disheartened, I became more and more unhappy with my whole life in Copenhagen. I even became unhappy with Klavs.

We had become incredibly close, dreaming and planning our future life in London together, but I was starting to realize that I was no longer sure about his commitment to dancing going forward, and began to think that he wasn't meant to be part of my future at all. I was totally overwhelmed by my feelings. I didn't know what to do with them. I felt like I had met the right guy, but I'd met him ten years too early. The thought of our being together forever started to freak me out.

Breakdown

When all these complex feelings about the judges, about Klavs, about where my life was going, were spinning round and round in my head, my mother came to Copenhagen on a visit. As soon as she saw me she knew at once something was wrong. 'Camilla,' she said. 'If you're not happy tell me and I'll take you straight home.'

I burst into tears and couldn't stop. All the feelings I'd been bottling up, hardly even acknowledging them, came flooding out.

The very next day she came with me to Klavs's house and we packed up all my stuff. Mor must have told his mum what was happening and why. I was in shock, in absolutely no state to do so. I cared so deeply for that lovely family that there was no way I'd want to hurt them. And even though I didn't want to hurt Klavs, he must have been broken-hearted by my sudden disappearance from his life.

It took me a year to come to terms with what I'd done. Once I had, I made a special trip back to Copenhagen to apologize and try to explain myself. They couldn't have been nicer about it.

Leaving my life in Copenhagen, upsetting Klavs and his wonderful family was no easy thing for a 19-year-old girl to do, but it taught me several lessons. I'd found out the hard way that I'm not superhuman, that I do get tired, and that winning was not the be-all and end-all if it wasn't making me happy. I'd learned I could say, 'Enough is enough. I can't do this anymore.' These were all vital lessons that were to shape my life, but I would find myself in similar situations again before realizing I should listen to my gut feeling: that when my soul is unhappy, I need to change something in my life. I have come to believe that the same or similar challenges will present themselves over and over again until we learn the lessons we are meant to learn from them.

IT'S NEVER TOO LATE TO SAY YOU'RE SORRY

When I went back to apologize to Klavs's family, I learned another life lesson that was just as important as the others. And that's sometimes we make decisions that we don't fully understand or that feel out of our control. Those decisions can be hurtful to other people, but it's never too late to apologize to them. When you realize you've made a mistake, go back, say sorry and explain. I had to tell Klavs's family that my decision to leave had nothing to do with them, that I was simply overwhelmed and overtired and couldn't cope any more. If I hadn't done that they might always have wondered if they'd done something to upset me. Of course they hadn't.

Starting over

So there I was, at my parents' house, back to square one. Although I was disheartened with the business, I was still missing dancing and started looking for a new partner, although after Klavs, I couldn't imagine I'd ever find anyone I'd dance so well with.

But, if there's a constant thread to my life, which you'll find out as you read my story, it's that in situations like that, someone else has always come along – and when they have it has never felt like I'm settling for second best. I tried out with a couple of boys, and even partnered a British one for a while. We actually went to a summer dance camp when I was back in Aalborg and I met Lars, a lovely Norwegian college boy there. I had a huge crush on him and was really happy when we started dating with no thought of dancing with each other. But when my coach suggested him as a prospective partner, I was more than keen. I even said I would move to Norway to dance with him.

I needed to live exactly how everyone else my age seemed to live

Lars was one of those lucky people who are simply naturally talented. And not only was he one of the best dancers I'd ever been paired with, he even shared my passion for Latin, which I'd put on hold during my years with Klavs. When Lars came into my life, it was as if the partner I had always looked for had finally arrived. But, he was coming to the end of his college days and although we had started planning our future and me actually moving up there, he decided to prioritize differently and go to university, so our partnership never really got off the ground. I felt as if I'd hit a brick wall.

Coming after all my growing disillusionment with the dancing world's politics and the grief I felt about leaving Klavs and his family, Lars going to university was the final straw. He was such a great dancer that I'd truly believed he was the one I'd make my name with. But when he gave up, I suddenly decided I'd had enough, too. It was as if the years I'd sacrificed in my childhood had finally caught up with me. I didn't have the energy to look for another partner and start afresh. 'That's it,' I yelled at my mother during a particularly dramatic scene that blew up one day in our kitchen in Aalborg. 'I never want to dance again!' And opening the kitchen bin, I threw my dancing shoes into it in a melodramatic gesture that could have come straight from a bad movie, shouting, 'And I won't be needing these any more!'

When I'd done that before I was five years old, Mor had known not to cancel my dance classes and tell my partner Torben to find someone else. This time was different. She knew better than to even think about dissuading me.

This time, I was 19, and my life for almost as long as I could remember it had been one long treadmill of work, work, work, then more work. There was no alternative route if I was to make my dreams of being a successful dancer come true. If you don't work hard at it, you've got no chance. And though I had never regretted a minute of it – even the exhausting extra training sessions I jumped at whenever I could – now I felt I was done with it. With Lars off the scene, I couldn't see any future for me in dancing and despite all the time, effort and money my family and I had invested in it, I didn't feel any regret as I called round my coaches to explain that I wouldn't need a new partner because I was giving up, too.

Maybe that seemed impulsive and rash, but I have never regretted it. I needed that time away from dancing to grow up, to really get to know myself and understand what I was all about. For years, to follow my dreams, I had sacrificed partying, friends, family, and basically my whole life. Now I needed to just enjoy myself and not have the constant pressure of rushing from college to training, or forever planning for the next competition. I needed to live exactly how everyone else my age seemed to live. I went to parties. I hung out at cafés. I dated boys who weren't on the dance circuit. It was fun and I wouldn't go back and change that time for the world.

In years to come I would wonder if having had that time to let my hair down, something Brendan never had, could in some way have contributed to our break-up because we weren't on exactly the same path.

When I met the man I was to marry, Kevin, he told me he'd done lots of partying in his life. I was thrilled because I knew he would never be worrying that he'd missed out on something!

DECISIONS, DECISIONS ...

As you can see, I made some very difficult decisions in my teens – leaving Klavs, and giving up dancing. I wish I'd known about this classic NLP exercise at the time. It really helps you to find out if the decision you're contemplating is the one you truly desire. I recommend you try it whenever you face a dilemma of some kind in your life.

With a specific question in mind, in this example about taking a year off abroad, say, 'Should I go travelling for a year?' Go through the model below, step by step, writing down your replies to each question.

1. What will happen if I don't? For the example above, the answer could be, 'If I don't go abroad and travel I will regret it later in life or I will be without those memories.'

2. What will happen if I do? You may say, 'If I go, I'll feel proud of myself for travelling on my own and I'll come home feeling inspired and happy having fulfilled one of my dreams.'

3. What won't happen if I do? You might answer, 'I won't have any regrets of what might have been.'

4. What won't happen if I don't go? Maybe your answer will be something along the lines of, 'I won't come home feeling excited' or 'I won't have spent my savings.'

Try the same exercise for all sorts of different scenarios, for example, 'Should I stay in this job?', 'Should I start exercising?', 'Should I give up smoking?' You'll usually find it's much easier to reach a decision once you have answered all four questions and seen your answers to them written down. The intention behind why we want to do certain things also becomes more apparent, which helps us in a decision-making situation.

CHAPTER 7
A NEW LIFE

When I gave up dancing, I had absolutely no intention of EVER going back to it, and for two years I lived my life as if dancing had never been part of it.

I fell in love with my first non-dancing boyfriend, Steen, a gorgeous man who worked in banking and I revelled in my new grown-up life with him; living in Copenhagen, going out as a couple, and talking to friends about our futures in business that we dreamed about. I loved the feeling that I was reinventing myself. When I met people I was Camilla, not Camilla the dancer. I was leading a new life – and it was fun.

Promises, promises

Ever since I'd modelled at the big fashion fairs in Copenhagen, I'd wanted to work in fashion retail. I loved clothes and the company I'd modelled for had promised me a position in their store. I knew their stock and had helped out in their Copenhagen branch when I'd lived there with Klavs. But by the time I finished college a few things there had changed, and they no longer had a vacancy for me.

I felt so let down and deflated – frustrated with the rejection after having been promised a job and then it not materializing. But I'd always been taught to pick myself up and brush myself down, so I just started looking for another job in fashion. And

I looked, and looked, and looked – I lost count of the number of jobs I applied for – and all I got was rejection after rejection.

Thinking outside the box

I was starting to despair when my Far noticed an ad in the local paper for a position in a well-known estate agency outside Copenhagen. It hadn't occurred to me to learn about selling anything other than clothes at that point, but I thought 'nothing ventured, nothing gained' – another cliché that has shaped my life – and I was really blown away when I was offered the job.

I learned a major lesson from this experience – and it's one that has since helped me many times throughout my life. Sometimes we can want something so badly that we feel completely devastated when we don't get it. I'd been shattered by all those rejections from the jobs I'd applied for in fashion. At this point in my life I was 100 per cent convinced that I was destined to work in that industry and I couldn't understand why I kept banging my head against a brick wall. When Far taught me to think outside the box and look at other opportunities I realized that there are times when we focus so much on what we have lost out on that we become blind to all the other things we could be doing instead. But it was much later in life that I realized that, in fact, it was the universe trying to open my mind and guide me in a different direction. The education I got from working in the estate agency was so much more valuable to me later on when I was running my own business. I looked back at this time in my life and thought, 'How funny: there I was getting terribly upset about what I couldn't have, but as soon as I made that mental shift in direction everything I really needed fell into place. It's a lesson you can learn, too. I believe in working toward the things you want from life. As I said at the very start of this book, nothing comes purely by chance. I also believe that you can work too hard toward a goal and if you're feeling as if you're constantly

Nothing comes purely by chance

pushing yourself but not really getting any nearer to it, then that can be a sign that you're heading in the wrong direction: you need to stop and turn back.

As my husband often says, 'Chase it and you'll chase it away.' What he means is don't squeeze all the air out of a situation. You need to leave some room to breathe and look around. Your dream may come true in a way that you hadn't previously imagined. Sometimes there's a bigger plan for us than the one we've become so focused on.

Things aren't always what they seem

On paper the job was with one of the most successful estate agencies in the country, in a very sought-after area north of Copenhagen – but, best of all, it came with the promise that as well as learning all the ins and outs of the day-to-day running of the business I'd be selling apartments, which was exactly what I wanted to do.

Sadly, once I'd started the job, it became pretty clear that other people working there had been made the same promise and it hadn't happened for them – and it wasn't going to happen for me either. But that wasn't the only problem: my boss was very highly strung! Everyone was terrified of her. Whenever she came in to the office, a ripple of fear always cut through the laughter and chatter that can make office life so enjoyable. She may have been a super-successful business woman and very good at her job, but she was volatile and fiery and if she lost a set of keys it was everyone's problem. She'd have all of us scurrying around like headless chickens trying to help find them. She'd shout and scream, flail her arms around, quite often with the slightest provocation.

Going to work made me feel sick with fear: I dreaded finding myself in her firing line. And then, one day I did. The trigger was a problem with the photocopier, which meant the pile of papers I had left on her desk was not perfect – and she demanded perfection. There's nothing wrong with that, of course, but sometimes compromise has to be the order of the day. But compromise was not a word in her vocabulary. She went wild. Nobody, and I mean nobody, had ever spoken to me the way she did then.

Respect yourself

I was close to tears but I suddenly snapped. I thought, 'Hang on. Stop and respect yourself: this woman's behaviour is out of order.' And before I knew it, I was saying it out loud. 'Why don't you do it yourself? I no longer work for you!' And, with that, I walked out of the door. She was shouting at me to come back and do my job, but I'd realized from past experience that feeling miserable and unhappy in my soul, as I was in that job, was something that could make me ill in the long run: I knew my past illness with pneumonia had been caused by stress.

Financially, of course, it was a gamble – I knew I couldn't really afford to give up this job and I wasn't sure if I would be able to find another estate agency who would take me on as an apprentice and let the time I'd already served count. I'm sure my parents thought it was foolish of me to jeopardize my career like this. But when I explained it to them, they started to understand. I valued how I felt above the money and when I look back I still feel proud of myself for setting those boundaries. It felt good to have shown myself that respect. The experience taught me that it's quite acceptable to say, 'Sorry, this isn't for me,' and I often talk to clients about setting the same kind of boundaries in order to regain their own self-respect. I'm sure most of us have been in situations at some point where we want to say, 'No, sorry, I haven't got the time to do that' or, 'I really don't fancy going to that.' And then somehow we've blurted out, 'Sure, no problem,' only to regret it and ask ourselves why we didn't just say, 'NO!' If you recognize this as something you do, you need to ask yourself: 'Am I setting boundaries?' And if you aren't, you may want to address this and start by saying no to other people. By learning to say it, you learn to set boundaries.

Rewards

I took a chance by quitting but I think I was rewarded for my courage and self-respect, because when I applied to three other agents in the area, they all offered me jobs – and the one I chose was with a company headed by a kind-hearted, charming and talented guy called Jesper. Working for him, I had the best time I could have wished for. He taught me so much and remains a dear friend to this day.

I don't want to even imagine how things would have panned out for me if I hadn't changed jobs. The thought of having two miserable years instead of two such rewarding ones is unthinkable. With Jesper I even ended up selling apartments, which is what I wanted to do. This whole experience was proof that it's worth following your heart for the sake of your happiness. It also proved to me that if you are not happy about something you can either stay and moan about it or take the bull by the horns and take some action. If I had stayed in that first job I would have been so unhappy, I'd have probably made other people around me unhappy talking about how miserable I felt. But instead of dwelling on everything that was wrong I decided to look at the options I had: to stay, or to leave. Staying would make me desperately unhappy – but leaving had the potential of making me happy if I found another job, so that's what I chose to focus on.

The job also sowed seeds for my future. Jesper taught me about contracts, mortgages and customer care – but most importantly about how best to communicate with colleagues. Along with having worked with a partner from the age of six, and later in *Strictly Come Dancing* having to work in bigger teams, this has really helped me in my current coaching career when I often advise others, individuals or groups of businessmen, how to communicate as effectively as possible.

Dilemmas

Toward the end of my apprenticeship, Jesper sold the business to two equally great guys who were now my bosses and who

I enjoyed working for just as much as I had for Jesper. They asked if I'd like to stay on in the same office as a certified estate agent once I'd served my apprenticeship and was fully qualified. I was now 21, and flattered to be asked. But the question made me suddenly realize that the rest of my life was about to be mapped out for me: I would rise through the ranks as an estate agent. I might be hugely successful at it – but was it what I really wanted? Ever since I was little, watching English and American TV, I'd dreamed of living in an English-speaking country. And, when I'd been dancing, I'd hoped it would help me to do this. All those dreams I'd had with Klavs about living in London were still burning away deep inside me. He was now in my past, but England or the USA were still part of my future, I could feel it. I'd thrown away my dance shoes, but I still wanted to be doing something I loved in one of these countries.

The company wanted a decision from me pretty soonish, but I was still dithering when, listening to the radio at Steen's house one night, a samba-style tune came on and I found myself up on my feet dancing along to it. I thought, 'Hang on a minute! Am I really done with all this?'

Soon after that a Latin American World Championship was being held in Denmark and, after two years of not wanting to engage in anything dance related, I decided to go along as a spectator. Sitting there, watching the competitors – most of whom I knew – giving it their all on the dance floor fuelled that feeling that maybe I wasn't as through with dance as I'd told myself.

No regrets

A few days later I remember thinking to myself, 'When I'm 30 and look back at my life what would I like to have achieved?' I asked myself to imagine my life in ten years' time if I took that estate agency job. I would probably have a comfortable lifestyle, a nice house, a car and money in the bank. On the other hand, if I went back to dancing, I would travel the world, live in the countries I'd dreamed about, learn about other cultures and live life on the edge. Maybe it wasn't too late to revive my dream of one day being one of the best Latin American ballroom dancers in the world or even to become an actress.

TRY THIS ...

1. Imagine yourself ten years further on in your life from where you are today.
2. Start writing a letter to yourself listing at least ten things you have achieved. It can be as simple as, 'I loved my visit to Italy,' or, 'When I picked up the phone in my new office in Manhattan.' Well if you are living in Birmingham and you are writing about an office on Broadway, couldn't that be telling you that perhaps you have some secret dreams that you want to follow?
3. Be as detailed as you can be in this letter as if everything you are writing to yourself has already happened, let your imagination run away with you.
4. Take a good look at what you have written and ask yourself honestly: what changes, if any, are needed to make some or all of this possible.

For me, well I looked at the letter I'd written to myself and realized that if I stayed sitting at my desk in Hellerup, just outside Copenhagen, I would not be travelling the world and performing on stage and TV or being interviewed for magazines.

Back to dancing

Doing that exercise led me directly to asking a few of my former coaches whether they thought I had been out of dancing too long to go back. Thankfully they didn't seem to think so and one of them even suggested I should call a British dancer I used to compete against in the UK as he was apparently without a partner. I knew of him, not just because we had been competing against each other ever since we were 12 at Blackpool Tower, but I seemed to recall that we'd been pen pals and even held hands a few years later and quite fancied each other! Anyway, I knew exactly who he meant.

'Why don't you call him?' my coach asked. 'See if he's still available for a try out?' That's when a dance couple meet up for the first time to see if they are compatible physically and mentally. It's kind of like going on a first date but on the dance floor and without any thoughts of romance. You feel nervous and excited all at the same time.

I had always thought Mark was a great dancer, and to be honest I secretly fancied him, so without any further consideration I decided to leave this decision, which would hugely affect my future, entirely up to fate. My thinking was this: I would call Mark and if he had not found a partner I would fly to London and try out with him. Hopefully it would all work out with us and I would move there. If he had already found a partner, I would take that as a sign that I should stay in Denmark and take the job at the estate agents instead.

Now it may seem mad to leave such a big decision up to the universe, but this is exactly what I did and to be honest it seems that the universe, or fate, or whatever we call it, had a pretty amazing plan for me.

ASK FOR A SIGN

Ask the universe to help you with whatever dilemma you face. I even ask out loud. I say, 'Please can I have a sign that xxxxx is the right decision for me to take.' A sign usually comes back pretty quickly: for example, an email might pop into my inbox or someone will call me with something relating to the issue I've just asked about. I bet that at some point in your life most of you have thought that you must call someone and almost at once the phone goes and it's that person ringing. I call this being in tune, being aware, simply noticing your thoughts, and I think that when you can do this you will find it easy to tune into the signs that the universe sends to guide you toward the right path.

Decisions in life

So I called Mark and he sounded very happy to hear from me but unfortunately he had found a partner a week earlier. I was just about to hang up, thinking, 'OK. Thanks Mark. That's it. My decision's made for me,' when he suddenly said, 'But hang on a minute, I have a flatmate who's looking for a partner. Why not try out with him?'

His name was Brendan Cole.

CHAPTER 8
MEETING MY MATCH

So there I was. I'd metaphorically tossed a coin. Heads – Mark saying he'd dance with me, and I'd be flying to England to revive my dancing career. Tails – Mark saying he wasn't free after all and my future would be as an estate agent. It could have gone either way and I really did think I would be equally happy with either outcome, but I just couldn't make the decision for myself. But Mark saying, 'Hang on a minute. I have a flatmate who's looking for a partner. Why not try out with him?' wasn't on either side of my imaginary coin. Even so, it seemed something that was meant to be and I immediately booked a flight to England for a try out with the mystery dancer. Little did I know, as I boarded that plane to London, what a pivotal role Brendan Cole, who like me had been out of dancing for a while and wanted to get back into it, would come to play in my life …

Not my type

Unlike Mark, who I'd always quite fancied, I didn't think Brendan was my type. But he was tall, with very fair skin, tight curly brown hair, and a good physique – nice-looking, I could see that, but he wasn't the sort of guy to make my heart skip a beat.

Physically, though, we were perfectly compatible as dancers – he was six feet tall, I was four inches shorter, and we were both long-limbed. So in theory at least, we'd look good together on the dance floor. These four inches were important. In the past I'd danced with boys who were shorter than me, and that really did look awkward!

And when Brendan and I started to chat, it was immediately obvious how much we had in common, especially when we simultaneously blurted out the names of coaches we'd like to work with. They were the same. We both hugely admired Donnie Burns and Gaynor Fairweather, who were the current Professional World Latin Dance Champions. They were stunning dancers: no wonder they won that title 16 times! Like us, they were tall and long-limbed. It was amazing to discover that Brendan and I had both been watching them on video, he in New Zealand and me in Denmark, both of us dreaming of one day working with them.

Then we stopped talking, started to dance, and from the moment our hands touched I knew we were a perfect match. Just like with Kenneth, Klavs and Lars, it just felt so right.

We started with my favourite dance, the rumba. As it's the slowest of the Latin dances, it's easy to get an idea of how you work together when you dance it. You can quickly see how he leads and how you follow; and how you both connect, mentally as well as physically.

We were about 15 minutes into it when suddenly I got this stabbing pain in my chest, as if there were knives in my heart. I knew I needed to breathe into the pain for it to go away, but I couldn't because that made it hurt more!

I was so embarrassed when I had to say, 'Excuse me – I have to lie down for a minute. I have pains in my heart!' It's little wonder that this became one of the defining jokes of our early relationship, something we would laugh about over and over again for years to come.

Fortunately I managed to pick myself up and continue with the try out – and by the time we'd finished I knew I wanted to go back to dancing, with Brendan as my partner.

No more politics

Having been disenchanted with the politics of the dance business in the past, I promised myself that this time round I would not let them concern me, I'd simply keep my mind on the dancing, and maintain a positive frame of mind at all times. I wanted to enjoy every step of my journey and if I ever found that this wasn't happening, I'd quit and do something else. I don't think I really realized at the time what a huge promise I had made that day, for trust me, it would be tested many times in the next ten years!

We both wanted to start dancing together straight away if we were to stand any chance in the upcoming Open British, to be held in Blackpool. But I still had three months of my estate agency apprenticeship to complete back in Copenhagen. If I left Denmark before that, I'd lose everything I'd worked for. If my dancing career didn't work out, I'd have no plan B career to fall back on. So Brendan, who didn't speak a word of Danish – how many people do? – said he would move over to Copenhagen.

I was blown away when he made that commitment – clearly this gorgeous, athletic-looking man was as keen as me to get back on the dance floor as soon as possible.

'Come and live with me!'

There was a lot to think about, practical things like what would Brendan do for money? And where would he live? In the end, I said, 'Come and live with me!' despite the fact that my flat was tiny, just a studio. It meant Brendan would have to sleep on a little fold-out bed I had, but as we so wanted to dance together, it seemed the only way. And it would only be for three months because we knew that if all went well with the Open British, the next step would be to move to London, where all the best dancers trained.

Dancers, like all sportsmen, often have to go through a lot of hardship when they decide to follow their dreams. So poor Brendan had to swallow his pride and take the only job he could get as a non-Danish speaker: he cleaned offices, cinemas and restaurants at night. He hated it and was earning less than £10 an hour to put toward our food and dance expenses. But we needed every penny we could get. A dress could cost anything from £500–£2,000. Trousers for the man cost £150 and shirts can be £150, even more if they're decorated with Swarovski crystals. A pack of them would easily be £50 and one pack didn't go far!

We'd chosen to train with a Danish coach called Karin Witander and the Australian champions Jason Roditis and Tonia Kosovich, and were working with one or other of them every day from six o'clock, when I finished work, until very late at night when Brendan had to go off to his cleaning jobs.

Falling in love again

The two of us would hang out together every day, eating together, training together, and going out together with my friends – who, fortunately for Brendan, all spoke English. They all kept asking, 'How come you're not a couple? You get on SO well!'

But back at home we'd lie at opposite sides of the room, he on his narrow fold-out bed, me on my ordinary one – with a sofa and a table between us – chatting until we fell asleep. Then one night as we lay there, we started talking about how we enjoyed each other's company but how complicated it was to date your dance partner and I just came out with the words, 'But I don't like to sleep alone …' and he said 'Neither do I!' And, from that night on, we no longer slept alone – even though we hid it from my parents in the early days, by making up Brendan's fold-out bed when they visited!

Back to Blackpool

We were really excited about going to Blackpool to compete in the Open British, the competition we'd been training so hard for. To the ballroom dance world it's what Wimbledon is to tennis.

There were 250 couples in the competition and having both been off the dance floor for quite some time, we were thrilled to make it into the last 98 and we only just missed getting into last 48. We were also delighted by the compliments from people saying how well-suited we were. We could see our future ahead of us and we were so thrilled about it.

With Blackpool under our belts, we were ready for that move to London, more specifically, south London, which was where most of the top trainers lived and had studios. There were champions from all over the world teaching there and couples would travel a long way to practise and take lessons with them. We wanted to train in one of the most famous dance studios – the Semley in Norbury – and to be inspired and surrounded by the champions who were there every night. The studio even had its own DJ who played all the latest dance tunes. Even just being there, you could feel the energy of all the champions whose careers the studio had shaped.

Not what I expected!

If by moving to south London I thought we'd be living and breathing the world of dance, I was wrong. It's a good job that I'd decided to stay positive through thick and thin before leaving my life in Denmark, because arriving in London and starting from the bottom was going to be tougher than I'd ever imagined.

I was leaving behind a job with good prospects, as well as my lovely little flat. But I'd decided to sublet it furnished, just in case I had to run home with my tail between my legs. And I'd also checked that a door would be left open at the estate agents. My Mor had wisely always told me not to burn all my bridges. I had my education to fall back on too, thanks to Far who'd persuaded me to do that course at business school and then the apprenticeship – so I'd always have something behind me if things didn't work out. But when I left Denmark I was full of hope and was convinced that I would need neither the flat nor the job again.

In that short time together, Brendan and I managed to save up enough to buy a brand new car, which we loaded with my things and after a special breakfast with my family at my sister Jeanet's house, we drove from Copenhagen to Jutland to catch the ferry to Harwich.

A new life

As we waved goodbye, my thoughts were a mixture of hope for the future and sadness at leaving my sister, Mor and Far behind. Jeanet and I had always been close, but she tended to be far less emotional than me. Telling me she loved me didn't come that easily to her, but just as we were about to leave, she handed me a card. As we drove away I opened it and the words I read brought a lump to my throat. 'I love you, Camilla,' she'd written. 'Always remember that – and know that you can always come home if you need to.'

I had to wipe away a couple of tears, as her words brought home to me what a big step I was taking, and how it would impact on my family as well – it wasn't just my life that was about to change. As my Far said in his speech at my wedding many years later, 'When Camilla left Denmark, she left a big gap in our hearts.'

We'd arranged for somewhere to live in London – the spare bedroom in a friend's parents' house not too far from the dance studios. It was lovely of them to put us up while we settled into London life, but having lived on my own for two years, I found it really difficult to share their bathroom and kitchen. It was like being with our parents again, so I made it my mission to find us our own flat, and within a month we'd found a small place in Norbury, a suburb in south London. It was very different to what I was used to in Copenhagen where I'd lived near water and lots of green parks, but it was convenient for all the dance studios, and at £500 a month it was affordable.

'When Camilla left Denmark, she left a big gap in our hearts'

We had a living room and a bedroom with only the most basic furniture in it, just a bed and a wardrobe. And it stayed with just a bed and a wardrobe until Brendan found bits of timber and built us some furniture. Back home in New Zealand he'd done some roofing, and he was the kind of practical guy who could turn his hand to pretty much anything he put his mind to, so fitting out our flat wasn't too hard for him. I loved that he could do all the things I didn't have a clue about. But I was good with the paperwork and finances, so we complemented each other well.

Before leaving Denmark I'd fixed myself up with a job in a Danish candle store that had a London branch – in Hammersmith! How was I to know when I arranged our accommodation that the commute from Norbury to Hammersmith was horrendous. It took an hour and a half in each direction in crowded Overground and Underground trains and buses crammed with commuters. Oh how I yearned for Denmark where most people cycled everywhere.

All my life I'd dreamed of living somewhere like London, and now here I was and this was the reality of London life! But I was with Brendan and we were at that lovely stage of being newly in love. Having each other to lean on made it all bearable for both of us.

The job wasn't quite what I was used to back home, of course. I'd had to come in on the ground floor as a sales assistant, but I knew it would be a good way to improve my English. I just wanted to get sorted as quickly as possible so I could have a bank account and rent a decent flat, which we did.

Honesty doesn't always pay!

It wasn't long before I was getting restless at the candle store though, and started to try to get another job, with a similar level of responsibility to what I'd had back home. I went to some really good interviews and after one of them I was told I was on a shortlist of two. When I went for the final interview, I knew

I was really close to getting the job. But, when the employer asked, 'How much would it mean to you to get this job?' I knew I should have said, 'It would mean everything for me.' Six simple little words and the job would probably have been mine. But they just weren't true, and before I knew it I was saying, 'I would love this job and I will do my best. But I came here to dance, to fulfil my dreams, and that will have to take first priority!' Sitting in that interview I'd realized that of course my dancing came first! It was the reason I'd left everything I loved!

I'd always thought that honesty was something that employers would value above all else. Silly me. I never did get to be a receptionist in an exclusive car dealership in Park Lane.

The job would have given our finances a terrific boost, but I'm proud that I stayed true to myself and stuck with my dream. Maybe this was a lesson sent to show me that I was meant to make that commitment, to tell me not to put being financially comfortable first at this stage, because if I had chosen that job it might have got in the way of my dream and my training.

After that it was crystal clear to me that I needed a job with less responsibility, one where I could leave work behind as soon as I walked out the door. So I carried on applying for jobs closer to home and finally got one with Mulberry in central London, the company that makes the sort of luxurious handbags that were way beyond my means. At that time!

It was a lovely place to work, but the job didn't pay brilliantly and, when I was reprimanded for not dusting the shelves properly, I couldn't help wishing I was back in my wonderful office in Copenhagen with all the satisfaction of sorting out contracts and going to business meetings.

A different kind of life

Doing a job I didn't like and not being well paid, travelling in sweaty, rush-hour public transport for hours every day, living in what to me was a grotty little flat, no wonder I felt homesick and cried a lot. I hated being broke and even though I had Brendan to turn to, I missed my family and friends.

We were finally in the right place to get the training we needed – but we didn't have nearly enough money for lessons, and even if we had, we sometimes lacked the energy to leave the flat. Tired, frustrated and living on next to nothing, unable to do what we'd moved to London to do, it's hardly surprising that our relationship was more than a little strained at times.

Brendan had got a job as a builder, which he hated. It wasn't the hard work, it was having to get up very early, usually after a hard night's training, the low pay and working outside in cold, wet weather. But he was doing it for the sake of our career. And I loved him for it, even though there were times when we were both so tired and tense that stress got the better of us and we began to argue quite a bit.

Our relationship survived, but the little car we'd bought to drive to the UK from Denmark didn't ...

We had a really bad argument one night and the next morning we hardly said a word to each other before Brendan left to go to work. He was pulling out of our drive, fumbling with his seat belt, when another car slammed into him, smashing his head against the windscreen, which shattered with the impact.

The first I knew about it was when I heard an ambulance. Brendan was taken to A&E and apart from being cut and bruised was OK. The car was a write-off, though. That didn't matter. What was really important to me and had made me sick with shock was that Brendan had suffered like that, thinking that after the row the night before and the sullen silence over breakfast I may not have loved him any more. That taught me a lesson: never let the sun set on a quarrel.

Learning London social skills

Life was very hard when we started out in London. But however low I felt at times the thing that kept me going was that light burning inside me: the dream of what could be. Every day, walking down the street I would remember and visualize my dreams, simply imagine how it would feel once I got there and remember that there was a purpose for all the hard work we were putting in.

Brendan had lived in London before meeting me and knew more about the way Londoners behave toward one another than I did. And that was something I struggled with for a while.

If one of my colleagues said, 'Hey, how are you? We must go for a drink sometime,' I'd reply, 'Sorry, but I'm really busy with my training every night so I'm not sure that's going to be possible.' I didn't realize I was coming across as aloof or rude. To me it was just being honest.

One day, my manager, who was a really nice lady, took me aside and gave me a little education in London social skills. 'Camilla,' she said, 'when someone asks you out for a drink or something, just smile and say, "Thanks. That'd be lovely." You see, they're just being friendly. They don't really mean it. They don't expect you to say yes.'

'How can you tell if they really mean it?' I asked.

'Oh, you'll know!' she laughed.

That was so different to the way things were done in Denmark, but eventually I got the hang of it. I also learnt to say 'Please!' and 'Sorry!' much more than we do at home. Not because we're rude, we just don't say the words very much. Now I find it really nice and polite and when I'm in Denmark I use them a lot – in Danish, not in English – and people sometimes look at me as if I'm from another planet, which I find really funny!

Love and respect

As well as learning my way around London etiquette, I was also taught a lesson in communication by Shirley Ballas, one of the top dance trainers in the UK. Shirley had a son who trained at the same studio as us and she often came to watch him. She was such a superstar that we yearned to take lessons from her, and eventually we asked her about it. We were gobsmacked by what she said, 'I don't know if we will be able to work together.' And before we could ask why, she went on, 'I've seen the way you are together, and I don't like the way you speak to each other!'

She must have seen our jaws drop. 'You need to take a good look at yourselves,' she explained. 'You don't show each other any respect when you're training. You argue ... speak harshly to each other.'

I honestly didn't know that we were putting out such negative energy. We must have been awful. No wonder she didn't want to work with us. When she said we spoke like squabbling siblings, I knew she was right. When Brendan reached for my hand I'd go 'Wha-a-at?' We'd shrug our shoulders and roll our eyes at each other. If I gave him advice, he'd ignore it. And, I'm ashamed to say, when he spoke rudely to me, I didn't listen to him at all. I simply blocked him! Shirley said that off the dance floor we seemed to be really nice people, but on it ... that was a different story. Her words were like a wake-up call. To be told that we were so unpleasant with each other that one of the world's top teachers wouldn't take us on was a slap in the face. But it was a lesson we needed to learn. From then on, we started treating each other with much more respect, using a softer tone of voice, and talking the way we would like to be talked to. The good news was that it wasn't long before we noticed that we had much more energy. Even better was that when Shirley saw the difference in our behaviour, she agreed to coach us, and that had a dramatic influence on our dancing and our careers.

RESPECT YOURSELF ...

One thing you have to do in any relationship is to ask yourself
if there is mutual respect. If not, you have to do whatever you
can to put it there. For example: if someone speaks to you in
a way that you find unacceptable, or constantly ignores your
opinion about something, and if you want them to respect you
instead, you have to tell them that you don't find it acceptable.
To set boundaries, you will have to let them know that you
find their attitude is souring the relationship and tell them
how you want them to behave if it is to survive. Maybe you
know someone who is constantly putting you down about the
way you look. Tell them that you like the way you look (assuming
you do) and ask them to stop talking about your appearance.
Or maybe your boss is constantly contacting you out of office
hours in your free time at home or even on holiday. Of course,
modern life being what it is, many of us take work home and
we all want to be reasonable, but you must learn that just
because you've been asked, that doesn't mean you have to
do it. Find the self-respect to set the boundary. If you don't
respect yourself, why should anyone respect you? If you are not
able to establish mutual respect, then perhaps it's time to finish
the relationship, look for a new job, whatever. I truly believe
that mutual respect is the foundation – whether it's in love or
at work or any great relationship – because when we have
respect, we have a strong and wonderful platform to build on.

CHAPTER 9
HARD TIMES

My god, our was life tough back then. Brendan and I were both working so hard yet earning around £6.50 an hour each. Out of that we had to pay for private dance lessons that cost ten times as much. I may have been unhappy a lot of the time but I never gave up hope that our efforts would eventually pay off – though there were times when I came close: our first Christmas for example …

There we were, feeling utterly defeated sitting on the floor of our sparsely furnished living room, both wishing we could be with our families, but there was no way we could afford to travel home, and neither of us fancied ringing our parents to ask for money again. We both had our pride and we felt that we had asked for a lot already – money for food, money for lessons, money for dresses, money for Brendan's work tools, money for this, money for that – not something to make a couple in their 20s feel good about themselves.

I really didn't want my parents to have to make more sacrifices just to help us out, even though I knew they would. They'd done so much while I was growing up and it just felt wrong to keep asking. I also didn't want them to say, 'Honey why don't you just move back home?' Which I think they probably would have if they had known exactly how tough it was at times.

Time to call it a day?

Sitting there on the floor that Christmas, I remember telling Brendan we had a choice. 'We can either power through, have Christmas here and somehow believe that things will work out for us,' I said to him. 'Or we can break up and say goodbye. Get on with our lives separately, me in Denmark, you in New Zealand, and admit that this challenge was too big for us.'

It hurt me to say it, but that's how bad things were. We were seriously, *seriously* broke. Brendan hadn't been paid, as the man he was working for said he was in a bit of money trouble.

I'm not a quitter, never have been, so I knew I wanted to stay. But I just didn't know how we were going to make it work. We had huge debts and it looked to me that we had so little going for us, that maybe our dream wasn't meant to be after all. But putting our choices into words not only made them real, it made us realize just how much our dancing meant to us. So when we agreed that we couldn't give up, not now when we've come so far, the relief was palpable. We had to make it work, no matter what it took.

The moment we said it, I felt that Brendan and I became fully committed to each other: we were in this for the long haul – together. No matter what life threw at us, we'd throw it right back and move on, and that is exactly what we did. So, while many of our rivals gave up or changed partners over the next eight years, we weathered every storm and stayed together. And the storms that blew like hurricanes were the ones that brought us closer together as a team. And that's something that still makes me proud, even after all the terrible times that came later in our relationship.

Thank you, universe!

And then, just after we'd made the decision to stay, the loveliest thing happened and it was as if the universe had said, 'Everything is going to be OK.' Suddenly we got calls from Brendan's grandad and my grandma, both offering to buy us flights home to Denmark as our Christmas gifts from them. They wanted to treat us to Christmas with our families!

At a time when we had come so close to giving up, struggling financially and working really hard, being surrounded by our loved ones and eating delicious home-cooked food was just the tonic we needed. It gave us the strength to carry on. Overnight everything felt better and once again I started believing that anything was possible. I even began to dream of living in Knightsbridge, the exclusive part of London where I worked in the Mulberry store. I'd wander along Beauchamp Place, imagining what it would be like to shop in its expensive boutiques and wear the beautiful designer dresses displayed in their windows. The fact that I usually only had about £5, which had to cover my lunch, in my pocket at the time was irrelevant to me. A girl can dream, can't she?

Just as my coach Tor had taught me to visualize dancing perfectly until I really did it, I now found I could visualize the type of car I would drive (a Mercedes, which I did while doing *Strictly*); where I would live (in Chelsea's pretty little Walton Street, which I did, ten years later); and where I would shop (at Suzanne Neville in Beauchamp Place, where I would one day find my wedding dress). Deep down I always believed I would make it – Mor had always taught me to believe in myself, and I did.

Think yourself happy!

I've always known that money can't buy happiness – that's something that has to come from inside you. Even so, visualizing having these things was a way of making my dream of success seem more tangible. These dreams were my way of planting the seeds that would create the future I wanted, and they came true.

I love telling this story to people I coach – especially when they say, 'But the road is so long, I can hardly pay my rent, so dreaming about one day living in one of the most expensive areas of town or running my own business, or having a wedding dress made by a famous designer is surely out of my reach?'

And guess what I'd say, *'Not if you believe it, take steps toward it and want it enough!'*

The next thing I ask them is, 'How has not believing it worked out for you then?' to which most of the them reply, 'It hasn't!' So I say, 'Why not just give it a try then?'

Give and you shall receive

Here's something else I learned around this time – that the law of attraction can have a huge influence on our lives. And that the law of attraction is simple: *what you put out, you attract.*

Visualizing what I wanted from life seemed to bring it to me, and that was all very positive. But, as I was to discover, the law of attraction can work two ways – positively and negatively.

Here's an example of that. When Brendan and I were surrounded by other competitors, even though they were really nice people, I found it hard to make close friends with them as I knew that for us to go on to the next round, we'd have to knock some of them out. Now, some other *What you put out,* dancers like to compare notes about *you attract* their training regimes, but there was a time when I couldn't see how this would help me. I was scared I'd be giving away something that may have given them an advantage that would stop us from winning. I can see now how that fear was getting in the way of friendship. But what I didn't think of was the fact that when I didn't share, neither did they. I had stopped the natural flow, missing out on vital information that could have helped me to grow and succeed even faster. It was only as I learnt more and more about myself and how the law of attraction works that I started to realize I could share without giving all my secrets away.

THE LAW OF ATTRACTION ...

When I was learning about the law of attraction, I read that if you want to be successful you should surround yourself

---

with successful people. So Brendan and I started to hang out with champions outside of training – not just because they were champions, but because they were also extremely lovely people who were willing to share their expertise. We watched and learned from them by just being in their company. It helped the visualization process to see how people who had already made it lived and behaved, and it made the dream feel more accessible.

I really believe that if you're happy and positive you will attract positive situations with happy and positive people. If you're grumpy and moaning constantly then you will probably find yourself in a lot of situations you'd rather not be in, and surrounded by other unhappy people. Sounds familiar? For example, take a day when you're in a rush and forget to pay for your parking and you get a ticket. That would make some people immediately think that it's going to be 'one of those days', and because that's what they think, that's what it turns out to be. They get an unexpected phone call that puts them in a bad mood; they drop their wallet; they can't find their car keys. Could it be that they've attracted some of this? Maybe if they'd said when they saw the parking ticket, 'Silly me! My fault. Mustn't be in such a rush next time.' then they'd stay in a good frame of mind so that when the phone rings they're in a positive mood, less likely to be angered by it, which makes them less flustered when it's over and less likely to drop their wallet and lose their keys.

Here's a way to test the law of attraction for yourself. Next time someone is rude to you, stop and take a look at yourself and notice how you are feeling. You may notice that you are in a bad mood, or maybe worried about something. If so, change how you feel by thinking of something that makes you smile and feel good inside right away. Then speak to the person calmly and because you feel good inside, more often than not, you will notice they act more pleasantly, because how you feel has rubbed off on them and made them feel better, too.

Even so, there may be times when you simply have to remove yourself from the person and the situation altogether. Sometimes, someone can be reflecting a way you used to behave rather than how you do now, reminding you how it used to look when you reacted to something in a certain way.

Share and share alike

Now there's nothing I like more than sharing experiences and information (well, within reason!), because I think we are all here to help each other to grow and learn. I love it when a friend phones or emails me to tell me something exciting they have discovered or read. I hope I have the same effect on others when I share something with them – and this is why I wanted to share my story in this book with you, too. It's an awesome way to live; life becomes so much more interesting when we are open to this.

But before I had this epiphany, Brendan was virtually the only one I confided in. I think, being each other's best friend, lover and dance partner perhaps put too much pressure on our relationship. In the end it broke us, but it worked for eight years and I think without this single-minded commitment we may never have got to where we did.

For many of these eight years we were competing in a very tough and frustrating world, often against couples who came from countries that fully funded them, allowing them to focus on dancing all day, every day. With everything paid for they spent their lives taking lessons and going to the gym, so they had loads of energy to put into their sport.

I never felt bitter toward them, but I used to yearn for the day when Brendan and I could devote our days to our passion just like them. But we both had full-time day jobs and could only practise in the evenings. We had to negotiate time off to take lessons and go to competitions, often abroad, on the weekends. And come Monday morning we were always expected back at work with smiles on our faces. Someone once asked me how on earth we kept going and why we didn't just give up. Friends used to be exhausted just listening to us telling them what our schedules were like. What they didn't know was that we were tired and short-tempered, and I was always run down, catching every cold or flu doing the rounds.

Shattered, I used to come home from work, throw myself on the bed, and watch a soap. I used to lie there, thinking how nice it would be not to move and just miss our training for once. But then I'd remember Mor saying, 'Yes you could do that – but how will you feel if you don't do well in your competition this weekend?' So, I'd have a quick power nap and pull myself together. I had made a commitment to myself, and although it was a struggle, I still had a dream – and little signs kept telling me I was right to keep going.

Remember I said that when Brendan and I first met we both dreamed of dancing like Donnie Burns and his amazing partner Gaynor Fairweather? They were our inspiration and we really looked up to them. Three years into our career together, we called and asked if they'd coach us – and we were beside ourselves with joy when they agreed.

Whenever they pulled over to give us a lift to class we saw that as a sign that they knew the hard times we were going through, that they knew what it was like to struggle – and that, one day, we'd get there, too. It was as if they were saying, 'Hang on in there, it will all be worth it.'

Something that really kept me going was this poem that Brendan's mum found and sent to help him through the hard times. I put it on the wall and used to read it every day – and I still read it now if I ever need cheering up.

Keep Going

When things go wrong, as they sometimes will,
When the road you're trudging seems all uphill,
When the funds are low and the debts are high,
And you want to smile, but you have to sigh,
When care is pressing you down a bit,
Rest, if you must, but don't you quit.

Life is queer with its twists and turns,
As every one of us sometimes learns,
And many a failure turns about,
When he might have won had he stuck it out;
Don't give up though the pace seems slow,
You may succeed with another blow.

Often the goal is nearer than,
It seems to a faint and faltering man,
Often the struggler has given up,
When he might have captured the victor's cup,
And he learned too late when the night slipped down,
How close he was to the golden crown.

Success is failure turned inside out –
The silver tint of the clouds of doubt,
And you never can tell how close you are,
It may be near when it seems so far,
So stick to the fight when you're hardest hit –
It's when things seem worst that you must not quit.

—Edgar A. Guest

I love the last bit where it says it's when you are hardest hit that you must not quit! That was often how it felt if we had a bad result so I thanked the universe for those words. If I had given up at my first, third or fifteenth hurdle I would never have got to experience all these awesome adventures and meet all these lovely people I encountered throughout my life. And now, when I give my motivational speeches I always say that it took me 20 years to have an overnight success.

I, well Brendan and I, achieved that success through a lot of hard work and strategic thinking to get round the problems that our pitiful lack of money caused us.

Looking the part

When you reach a certain level as a dancer you're expected to wear new costumes for all the major competitions: it's not just your dancing that gets you through to the next round, you have to stand out. This means that grooming goes hand in hand with technical ability. But having to look great all the time put yet another strain on our tiny budget. We cut and coloured our own hair (something I'd learned from Mor who had her own salon, remember). I wore fake nails, too, to extend the elegant lines in our arm movements. In the beginning I stuck them on and took them off straight after the competition, but later on, when I could afford it, I had acrylics put on once a month. Then there was all the fake tanning – you would NEVER think of doing a competition without having fake-tanned first! That's not just because dancers like to look bronzed, it's because if you're *not* tanned your muscle definition disappears under the spotlights. With a tan, all your hard work is shown off better, especially in Latin where the girls' dresses are quite skimpy and men's shirts are often slashed to the waist.

I used to hate tanning and wearing fake lashes and nails – it was the one side of the sport I detested, but I'd had to do it from an early age, because, as Mor had always said, it wasn't worth losing points just because I didn't do all that stuff!

Brendan wanted the best for us too and, believe it or not, he actually became my couturier so I could wear the lovely dresses I needed but struggled to afford! That started after we'd paid someone else to make me a dance dress and Brendan was unimpressed with what she came up with. He begrudged the money we'd spent on something that wasn't really what we wanted – and especially so as we'd slogged so hard for that money in the first place.

Now Brendan is someone who can do practically anything he puts his mind to, so when he set out to prove he could make me a better dress, he was determined not to fail. 'If I can build a house, I can "build" a dress,' he said. And that's just what he did, although 'build' is not the word I'd have used.

We spent our next pay cheques on a cheap sewing machine, then he cut one of my old dresses apart in order to make a pattern and off we went to Brixton Market to pick up cheap fabric for him to test out his designs.

He soon worked out that if he could make a perfectly fitted body, a bit like a swimsuit, then he could drape and sew anything on top of it – and, I have to admit, he was brilliant at it. He received so many compliments for his designs that it wasn't long before he was making his own trousers and shirts, too. He was even asked by other dancers if he would make theirs, but he had his hands full with the number of costumes we needed.

HIDDEN TALENTS ...

Do you have a hidden talent that could maybe help you in your life to feel inspired or to get ahead in your career? Sometimes, by finding our inner creativity, our passion for life can be refuelled.

- To work out where your passion or creativity lies, write down what you are doing when you are the happiest. In my life the answer would be performing, being able to engage with an audience and being able to make an audience connect with their emotions through my performance, whether that's coaching, speaking or dancing.
- Look at what you wrote and see if you can narrow it down, maybe to a specific skill. Here I whittled it down to coaching clients, presenting, acting and speaking, and to inspire people to connect with their inner happiness. If you are thinking of making the skill (or skills) your job, start researching online to see what qualifications you need, and what courses are available. I've taken lots over the years, not just dance and performance courses but hypnotherapy and NLP ones, too. You can fit them around your life – at weekends and in the evenings and on holidays: that's when I did many of mine.

CHAPTER 10
TURNING PROFESSIONAL

The politics of the dance world are complex, and Brendan and I found ourselves caught in the middle of them.

We were dancing for Denmark, sometimes ranking third or fourth for my country, but sometimes not even making the final. That was bad, for if our career was to progress, we had to be in the top two – only then would we be invited to compete in the world championships. We were also missing out on smaller 'invitation only' competitions, which only wanted *one* couple from each country. These competitions mattered a lot because they paid for the dancers' travel *and* offered prize money. They also raised a couple's profile as they were seen more by international judges, so it's little wonder that we were so keen to take part in them.

We knew we were ready to compete at this level because after less than two years dancing together in the Blackpool competitions, which were open to anyone, our ranking had constantly improved and, ironically, we were often beating some couples ranked higher than us in Danish competitions.

We eventually decided the best way to move our careers up a gear, to be seen competing as much as possible, was to dance for another country. Denmark was my country. Brendan came from New Zealand. So why not try dancing for there?

He hadn't seen his family for two years, and was feeling really homesick, so it seemed like a no-brainer to go back to New Zealand, catch up with his folks, and try to win the championships there. If we could just pull that off, then we knew we'd soon be on our way – dancing for his country on the international dance circuit.

Family affairs

There was just one snag: we'd have to beat New Zealand's reigning champions. And guess who they just happened to be? Brendan's older brother, Scott, and younger sister, Vanessa! And they weren't just the reigning champions, they'd held the title for several years. In 1997, the year we planned to compete, they had split as dance partners, but we knew that Vanessa still wanted to hang on to her title, dancing with someone new. Scott wasn't going to be a problem for her as he'd not yet found a new partner. But how would she feel about her other big brother, Brendan, coming back and trying to knock her off her pedestal, and how would he feel about it? It was a big decision for Brendan.

After a lot of soul-searching on Brendan's part, we decided we had to put our career before family rivalry and, spurred on by making the top 24 in the Open British Amateur Latin at Blackpool the same year, off we went to NZ, hearts in our mouths about how it would pan out. With Brendan and I wanting that trophy every bit as much as Vanessa and her partner did, it's little wonder that emotions ran high and that we ended up barely on speaking terms with her.

I felt so sorry for Brendan's parents, standing helplessly on the sidelines, wanting both of their children to win, but knowing that could never be. They'd looked forward to seeing us for so long, and now everything was spinning out of their control. It felt just like *Strictly Ballroom*. I loved that film. I hated being made to feel I'd been in it.

Brendan and I did win the trophy, becoming the New Zealand Champions, a title we held for a number of years, while

Vanessa came second. There was a lot of hurt and animosity between us, but eventually we all got over it and were able to become friends again.

Enjoy the journey

New Zealand is one of the most beautiful countries in the world, and something about it sparked my inner spirituality and began to open up my mind. While I was there I realized that it was time to live and enjoy the journey to success, for the journey really is as important as the destination. How much we enjoy our day-to-day life really matters far more than a brief moment of success after years of miserable slogging.

Despite dancing for New Zealand, we were still based in London because of its access to some of the best dance studios in the world, but the truth was that although our dancing was getting better and better, life was taking its toll. While some countries allowed their amateur dancers to earn their living by coaching students, New Zealand didn't, so we couldn't give up our day jobs. And, after three years of standing up all day in the Mulberry store and then training all evening, I was exhausted.

Thinking about enjoying the journey and loving the day to day, I knew I had to find something else and finally took an office job in a call centre that needed Danish speakers.

Brendan, who was just as worn out as I was, got a job with an insurance company. Both offices were near to home, saving us the time and money that we'd spent commuting – and, once I was sitting all day instead of standing, I couldn't believe how much more energy I suddenly had for dancing.

I soon negotiated a part-time contract in the new job, so I'd have more time for training and competing. But that meant money wasn't just tight, it was seriously lacking! I didn't know quite how to get the balance right between working the hours that we needed to get by financially and having the time and energy needed to spend on our dancing.

Debts and dilemmas

By this time, we had a £10,000 credit card bill hanging round our necks, which we'd run up trying to make it as amateurs. Now that we were New Zealand champions, we were getting lots of invitations to competitions around the world, and these invitations covered our travel expenses, but we still had to pay for our own travel to the other competitions we wanted to enter, and that was a constant struggle. We were living on beans and toast and simple pasta dishes, hardly the kind of sustenance athletes need, and dancers are just as much athletes as Olympic sprinters. Knowing what I know now about healthy diets, it's surprising we ever had the energy to compete.

Sometimes we'd even sublet our sitting room to Brendan's brother or friends if they were staying in the UK, just to cover the rent and bills as all our money was going on our dancing. There was one month when we were so short that we had to toss up between buying food or paying one of our coaches. We couldn't starve, so I called the coach to cancel our lesson with him.

I could hardly believe it when he said, 'Oh, don't worry. Just come along anyway and you can have the lesson on me.'

We both thought that was extremely generous. But at the end of the lesson he forgot what he'd said and asked for payment anyway. We were both too embarrassed to tell him that we couldn't afford it, especially as there were other people in the room. So I wrote a cheque, without having the foggiest idea of whether or not it would clear. To top things off, he suggested we jump in a cab with another couple who lived near us, and with our train tickets in our pockets, we got in the taxi. Another expense we couldn't afford!

Why didn't I say something? Two reasons. I put the coaches on a pedestal and I was scared about how they may judge me. And another dancer had once told me never let coaches know that you're hard up. We juggled our finances round and

You should only worry about what is in your control

borrowed on our credit cards and thankfully, when the cheque was presented for payment, there was enough in our account to clear it – imagine how mortified I'd have been if it hadn't – but I like to think that this experience taught me empathy, respect and an understanding of the fact that each person's situation is different. Our credit card debt was still mounting and once again we were seriously wondering how on earth we were going to carry on. We couldn't see how we'd ever raise the money to pay it back while also competing every weekend and it seemed that our only choice was to turn professional, which would allow us to coach other students for a living and also to enter competitions offering bigger financial rewards.

But it was a huge dilemma because normally only the very top amateur dancers turned professional. We were *near* the top, but we weren't *at the very top*. So turning professional would mean suddenly competing on a completely different level against many of the people who'd beaten us in the past!

Needing a miracle

We were still working out the pros and cons of going professional, knowing that we'd reached a turning point and that what we really needed was a miracle, when a miracle happened. At least that's what it seemed like to us when out of the blue a Chinese dancer who'd seen us perform at Blackpool called and asked us if we'd like to compete in Hong Kong around Christmas time. Did we jump at the chance, or did we jump at the chance? Not only would the organizers pay our travel expenses, not only was there prize money on offer, but there was a chance we'd be picked for future shows.

We didn't really know what to expect, but left London with a sense that new and exciting adventures were on the horizon. Little did we know at the time that this trip would inspire a big change in our career and help our journey to stay on track with our goals.

The studio in Hong Kong welcomed us with open arms, picking us up from the airport and arranging all our travel and accommodation for us. If that's how professionals were treated, it felt great!

A strange turn of events

Isn't it funny how fate can smile one day and scowl the next. Soon after arriving in Hong Kong, Brendan collapsed on our bathroom floor with agonizing food poisoning.

In a panic, I called another couple from New Zealand who I knew were staying in the same hotel. Sick with anxiety I explained what was happening and begged them to help me get Brendan to the hospital. 'No problem, of course we'll help,' they said, and, as a result of that terrifying experience, Richard and Natalie Perry became and remain very dear friends of mine.

For a week, I sat watching Brendan looking so ill, and praying that he would recover. Totally beside myself with worry, I turned to books for solace, reaching for anything I thought could calm and reassure me. One of the ones I read as I sat by Brendan's bedside was *The Celestine Prophecy*, which had a section explaining synchronicity – and how our paths cross with other people's for a reason. For example if missing your train and taking a later one leads to you meeting someone on the second train who comes to be important in your life, then that delay was meant to be. According to this book, fate controls our lives as closely as that – and we should not be scared of speaking to new people, because we have met them for a reason and more often than not they have information to exchange.

This led me to think that it could be no coincidence that we'd been invited to Hong Kong at a time when we were fighting a losing battle trying to make ends meet. It was no mere coincidence that I'd picked up that book and read about noticing the signs around us.

I started paying more attention to what people around us were saying and when someone from the Hong Kong studio asked if we'd like to return as professionals the following year, and then another ballroom couple suggested that they thought our style would suit the professional ranks better and, therefore, we'd be able to achieve better results, it seemed that our destiny was sealed. We should take a leap and turn professional.

When Brendan was better, I discussed it with him and we agreed that being treated like professionals in Hong Kong was a fate-given chance to see how our lives would be if we joined their ranks.

So we let the organizers of the Hong Kong event and the Dance Federation know that the competition we were about to dance there would be our last one as amateurs. And, if we needed another sign, two weeks later, and despite Brendan still not being 100 per cent recovered, we won the competition and so we immediately announced that we were now turning professional.

Aiming for the top 12

I was looking forward to a fresh beginning and I was so excited that I had butterflies in my stomach. Two months after we left Hong Kong, we'd be competing as professionals for the first time in the UK Open Championships, but before we got that far we had to field plenty of negativity from many a poor pessimist determined to tell us that very few couples had ever succeeded in going from the top 24 in the amateur world ranking into the top 12 professionals, which was where we were aiming to be within a year.

It wasn't the first time, and certainly wouldn't be the last, that someone would tell me it was impossible to do something. All I can say is, thank God I trusted my own instinct and didn't let these other people's limited beliefs get in my way. So far in my life, when I trust my instinct, it usually works out to be the right decision. Remember, if someone ever tries to tell you that something will not be possible for you, it's your life, so I find that your choice is always the best option when you are the one deciding which direction your journey should take.

We worked hard, which was especially tough for Brendan, who was only just getting his full strength back after his bout of food poisoning in Hong Kong. But we were determined to dance in the UK International Championship in Bournemouth. Our plan was to make the final of the Professional Rising Star (for newcomers to the professional circuit), and be in the top 12 in the Open Professional.

I was about to learn a very valuable lesson though. I put too much pressure on myself before Bournemouth, knowing that it was our first professional competition and feeling I had a lot to prove to all the doubters who said we couldn't do it. And instead of trusting that we had done enough training and preparation beforehand, I became over-focused on what the judges and the audience would think of us instead of just keeping calm and concentrating on what was in my control. As I had learned when I tried to get into a fashion career, but failed, sometimes you can want something so much that you squeeze it so hard that all the air, life and love is forced out of it.

That's exactly what I did in this particular competition. I wanted to succeed so badly that my nerves got the better of me.

Under pressure

I usually manage to harness my nerves and use the adrenalin to boost my performance. But this time, wow, the nerves got to me in a very different way. I could hardly dance – I felt as if my muscles had frozen solid and my mind was in pieces – and needless to say our professional career wasn't launched with the fanfare we'd wanted.

I was so annoyed with myself for letting my nerves get to me, and went through the whole day over and over again in my mind until I came to the conclusion that I'd been too wrapped up in trying to impress other people. Instead I should have concentrated on how I felt. It was me who had built up all this extra pressure and stress, and it did nothing to help me. It was a good way to learn though, and I decided that putting extra stress on myself and being nervous were not going to get me the result I desired. From then on, I knew that all I could do was prepare myself physically *and* mentally as well as I could, enjoy the moment, and trust in my own ability. If I hadn't already known that it was mind over matter in a competitive situation, I knew it now – 100 per cent. As my coach Tor had taught me years before: you should only worry about what is in your control.

Magic moment

Over the next five months, before the next major championship in Blackpool, we worked hard on our dancing, and enjoyed the travelling and teaching. We even went to Beijing and performed in front of thousands of people: our first big show! It was just us who were booked to entertain the audience in this huge arena and it was like a launch pad of what was to come. One dance especially stands out for me – our fourth one – the paso doble ...

I was lying on the floor under the cape, about to be dragged across the floor in Matador style, and, as Brendan walked out, I heard the audience's thunderous applause and screams of excitement. They were cheering and clapping so loudly that a wave of emotion surged through my body. Lying under the cape, I could feel tears welling up and I had to try really hard not to let them run down my cheeks.

The love this audience showed made me feel as if the universe was saying, 'You guys will be OK. Good things will come your way. This is just the beginning: your hard work will pay off.'

After that show, we knew we could not just entertain an audience, but hold it; and that became our selling point. We were technically good, but we were more than that. When we danced, we were telling a story, using the love and deep passion we shared for each other and for the art of dancing to build genuine emotion into it.

ANCHORING

Nowadays I help other people overcome their fears and nerves and it makes sense that I needed to learn this lesson back then. I often use this really simple anchoring exercise, which helps in situations when you don't want nerves to get the better of you, or you're preparing for something out of your comfort zone. You may find it helpful when you want to feel more energized, confident, calm or relaxed in a situation that looms in your life; indeed you may need all four of those emotions at the same time – in which case go through the exercise one emotion at a time.

I'll use 'calm' as an example below, but you can choose whichever emotion you wish to anchor. If it's more than one, I suggest you start with 'calm' and 'relaxed' and then build on them.

1. Start by closing your eyes and thinking back to a time when you felt completely calm. If you can't think of such a time, then think of something that soothes you, like the sea or even someone you know who always seems to be calm.

2. Recall the memory of calmness – you may get a picture in your mind or you may remember a sound or get a lovely feeling inside … If you can't think of an experience or person from your life, try a symbol of calmness – maybe a Buddha or a celebrity who conjures calmness for you.

3. As you recall this memory you will reach a point when the feeling increases and intensifies and then diminishes and finally disappears. The key is to anchor it when it's at its strongest. You can do this by, for example, pushing your index finger and thumb together when you feel the emotion at its highest intensity.

4. Test your anchor by pressing your thumb and finger together again – that action should bring back that deep feeling of calm. Your anchor is now ready for you to use at any time you need it. If it doesn't work after the first time repeat the steps above until the anchor works for you. Build up to four emotions on top of each other if you need to.

When we returned from Asia we trained and competed as much as we could before the Blackpool championships. We also tried to bring our debts down to at least some sort of manageable level, so we put all our stuff into storage and rented a cheap room in a friend's flat. Having had a place of our own, to be suddenly sharing a flat with four others, with just a flimsy cardboard partition between us and what was the rest of the flat's living space, wasn't easy! But we just got on with it and kept reminding ourselves why we were doing it.

Dancewise, we were getting good results especially in the lead-up competitions to the big one in Blackpool. Not just results – one teacher, who wasn't even ours, told us that the way we were looking, we should be aiming for the Open British Rising Star final, which is where any amateur just turning professional would love to be. A dancer's results at Blackpool works like a CV as most people in our business either go to dance there or read about the rankings afterwards, so that teacher's words were a big confidence booster – and another sign that we were doing the right thing.

RISING STARS

Things had changed after turning pro. We had this new, fresh approach and belief in ourselves. You know the kind of feel-good factor and excitement you get when you've done something nice for yourself, like getting your hair cut. Well, it was just like that.

Testing, testing

But then, with just four weeks to go before the prestigious Blackpool Open British – as I said before, the Wimbledon of the dance world and the competition we'd worked so hard for – fate stepped in and I was suddenly faced with a challenge that seemed to have been sent to test my commitment and determination.

When I was coming home late one evening after a competition, disaster struck. I was exhausted and fell over outside the house and got this shooting pain in my ankle. It was so painful I couldn't get up. I just lay there screaming in agony until Brendan heard me and ran out to pick me up. I'd had smaller ankle injuries, like sprains, in the past; but I knew this was different – it felt as if something had snapped. 'Please, God!!' I said to myself, 'Don't let it be my Achilles tendon.'

I called all the specialists I knew, including some of London's top physiotherapists and osteopaths, but no one would even consider seeing me until the swelling had gone down.

I wrapped my foot with ice packs to try to get the swelling to go down as quickly as possible, but the waiting was another agony, as I was desperate to get on with the healing and back on the dance floor. But when I finally saw one of the top physiotherapists in town, the news was grim. 'There's no way you'll be dancing in Blackpool,' she said. 'It'll take at least six weeks to heal. Your Achilles tendon is literally hanging on a very thin thread.'

I couldn't believe what I was hearing. There had to be a way, I was sure there had to. Brendan and I had worked so hard for the competition that I could *smell* the final. It was unthinkable that we wouldn't even be able to compete. So I kept going back to the physio for treatments, and also looked around for other people who could help me – and, finally, one osteopath said she could help! She realigned my whole body, from top to toe, working not just on my foot, but on my back and neck, too. As well as an osteopath, she was also a healer and was convinced of my body's ability to recover in time for the competition.

'Give it some more rest and a few treatments,' she said, 'and you'll soon be dancing again.' She was right. Three weeks later I was back on the dance floor.

Victim

So I was not to be a victim after all – my determination had paid off. My foot was strapped and it was painful, but the pain was manageable. Brendan and I were mentally and physically ready, and when the day came we competed against over 200 other couples, dancing for hour after endless hour.

But there had been one victim – and that was my dance outfit! During the stress we went through in the build-up to the competition, our hot tempers had got the better of us when I decided that the skimpy two-piece Brendan had designed for me was far too revealing. I don't like to flash my body inappropriately, so I prefer to keep my midriff covered.

In the row that ensued, the pieces ended up in the dustbin. We had to rescue them a few days later, and, after Brendan had altered it to make it less revealing, I wore it for the Rising Star final – and it was stunning.

As the judges whittled down the numbers through seven rounds, the atmosphere became more and more exciting. We saw ourselves go through to the quarter-final … then the semi-final … and then the grand final. We didn't win, but we came third.

It was an extraordinary day for us and the next morning when I woke up to a knock on our hotel bedroom door and the porter brought in a lovely bouquet of flowers from one of the studios in Hong Kong, I knew it really had happened and that it wasn't just a dream. We had danced our first final at the glamorous Winter Gardens Ballroom in Blackpool, an event I'd been dreaming of since my childhood. In an instant all the tears, all the struggle, all the rows seemed like a distant memory. No wonder I felt like singing Sinatra's 'My Way'.

Against all the odds, all our hard work had paid off

Three years later …

Three whirlwind years later – three years of living out of suitcases and seeing hotel rooms far more than we saw our own home as we performed all round the world, often in front of VIP audiences, and even at the Kremlin – we were back at the prestigious Open British again, and this time we made the top 12 in the world in all five of our dances – our best result in the Open British, although by then we'd made the semifinal in most other world class events. It was our proudest moment as, looking around, we were all too aware that most of the other couples on the floor with us had already been amateur world champions. Having never made the top 12 when we were competing as amateurs, to now be rubbing shoulders with the best in the professional ranks, we felt like we had finally made it. Against all the odds, all our hard work had paid off.

MY RECIPE FOR SUCCESS

I followed what I call a recipe for success in the Open British, compared to all the others I'd done before, and it's one that we can all apply when we have a goal to work toward – whether it is in our professional or private lives. Like all good recipes, it's got several ingredients:

1. Stop focusing on what other people are doing and focus on you at this particular moment in time. After all, the only thing in your control is you, not the circumstances or the people around you, but you. What your competitors/colleagues/friends are doing should not be your focus. Someone very wise once told me that energy follows thought. That means that when you are focusing on what others are doing you are wasting valuable energy on them, energy that you could be spending on yourself.

2. Make a sign saying, 'Energy follows thought' in big letters and put it on your wall, somewhere really conspicuous. This will remind you to stop and bring your thoughts back to you when they wander and you start focusing on others. The time you spend thinking and concerning yourself with other people's business is wasted energy: it's time much better spent focusing on your journey, learning, changing and growing. So, the next time you catch yourself doing this, realize what you're doing, stop it and immediately bring your thoughts back to you.

   Every time I looked at the sign I would repeat the sentence and I soon realized how much more time Brendan and I had to spend on ourselves at practice, rather than worrying about what our competitors were doing around us. The quality of our rehearsals improved tenfold. Imagine how much more you'd get done at work if all the energy you put into gossiping, worrying or stressing was used for working on your actual projects instead!

Have you ever been caught up in what others are doing at work, or been jealous at someone else's success? Now is the time to stop and start concentrating on how you can improve your life and your journey. Instead of being jealous about others doing well, why not see them as an inspiration, as someone who has shown you if it's possible for them, it's possible for you?

3. Plan and rehearse your success by making sure you have done everything in your power to be ready for the event – that you have rehearsed, trained and prepared. It could be a meeting, an interview, an audition, a marathon, anything at all. Just remember practice makes perfect and, as Benjamin Franklin said, 'He who fails to prepare, prepares to fail.'

4. Be in tune with your body and mind and listen to what they're saying to you. They will tell you when to push harder, when to ease off, when to sleep, eat and relax – so just get in tune with yourself. Maybe you're thinking, 'I can't do that, I don't know how?' – well, guess what, I didn't either, but I decided to follow what felt right to me and not to everyone else around me. One of the best pieces of advice I ever received was from someone who told me to go with my gut feeling. When something makes you feel unsettled or heavy in your stomach when you think about it, then it's probably not right for you. I find that when I make the correct decisions I feel comfortable, relaxed and totally at ease. It just feels right all round. Now, this is not to be used as an excuse for not pushing ourselves and doing something that's out of our comfort zone. It's important to go there sometimes, but being

uncomfortable there is different to doing something that doesn't feel instinctively right.

5. Build up a team of equally positive friends who'll support you and believe in you and your ability. You've got no time for those who are going to put you down or push their limited beliefs onto you. A long time ago, I read somewhere that it helps to be surrounded by people who are already successful at what you wish to do – it's inspiring! That's why I surrounded myself with friends who were already world champions and I made sure I went and trained in places where there would be more champions. I picked teachers and coaches who had done it already, who'd made it and who were not afraid to tell me the truth. And surrounding myself with experts who'll tell me when I'm doing something wrong or could do it better is something I still do when I'm learning something new. Let's face it, as lovely as it may have been for me to be told that what I was doing was amazing, no 'yes' person was going to help me grow and push my barriers! I needed someone who knew what it took to get to my goal. In the end though, team or no team, you have to be the one who makes the decisions because it's your life. So ask people for advice, gain as much knowledge as possible but make the major decisions yourself. That way, right or wrong, you will never look back and regret leaving your destiny to someone else.

6. Every time you think a negative thought, stop, rephrase it and change it into a positive one.

7. Eat right for your challenge. Weightlifters need bulk and muscle; tennis players need strength and stamina; sprinters need instant energy. Eating the right food helps them achieve and be strong, fit and healthy inside and out.

8. Exercise – no matter what job you are doing, it's important to exercise and feel physically ready for a challenge.

It makes you feel good and keeps you energized and up for any challenge that lies ahead. Even if the only time you can find to exercise is walking to work, then make that your walk of empowerment. Focus on your breathing and think positive thoughts like, 'I'm am strong, I am confident.' Some people prefer to say their mantras quietly out loud. Both ways work, so do the one that is best for you.

9. Meditate and reflect. Take from 5 to 20 minutes to 'just be' or go for a walk. Whatever you do, make it your time to focus on you. Sometimes I go for a walk or just sit in stillness and think about all the lovely people I have in my life, and in my mind I say thank you to each one. Other times I think about all the things I have to be grateful for in my life, and sometimes I simply imagine what it will be like when my dream will be a reality. Or I just sit and let all my thoughts evaporate and enjoy the calmness of just being completely still. I want to stress the fact that five minutes is better than nothing and can make a big difference to your life.

Pastures new

Six months after making that top 12, we were back in Blackpool – this time for the Closed British, in which couples compete to represent Britain in the World Championships – and it just so happened that there was a team of television producers from London who had come up to Blackpool to scout for talent for a new show, which was to be called *Strictly Come Dancing*.

All the competitors were called to a meeting, after which we'd each let the production team know if we were interested in auditioning. Then they would have a look at our performances and maybe get us in for a screen test back in London. I'd grown up watching the original BBC TV series *Come Dancing* – I had no idea how different this new show would turn out to be.

At this point, trust me, I don't think anyone had an inkling that the programme would turn out to be a worldwide success and that the concept would sell to over 30 countries, becoming known in many of them as *Dancing with the Stars*. But a few of us thought that it sounded like an exciting idea, though, and I knew I felt ready for a challenge – but I had no idea what I could be letting myself in for. How could I?

We were invited to ask questions about the show, so we'd be as fully informed as possible before reaching any final decision. 'Will dancing be displayed as a serious art or a sport?' someone asked. 'Will the programme help people to realize how much training and technique is involved in dancing?' asked someone else. 'That there's more to it than fake tan, false eyelashes and sequined outfits?'

We were promised that although the show was definitely going to be glamorous, it would also be educational about our sport. The audience would get to know the dance world and how hard we all worked for our passion.

Now I am very proud of the world I had grown up in, so when I heard that, I took a chance and put my name forward. And even though he was reluctant, I managed to persuade Brendan to put his name down, too.

And then someone, one of the top competitors, stood up and asked if anyone had thought that if the show really took off, the dancers could become celebrities in their own right. 'That,' she said, 'could make it extremely difficult to carry on as we currently do in the dance world. It may even make it impossible for us to return to our normal dancing lives! What happens then?'

Looking back, it was a very clever point to have made, but I don't think many of the people there actually thought that the show would get so big that we had to worry about that.

However, we were told that we may not be selected as couples, and that one of us may have to leave the other behind. Having not spent any time apart for eight years, having a joint email address and only one cell phone between us, this was a huge risk for Brendan and me to take. If that happened to us, it could mean a massive change to our lives. But we didn't even think about that.

Earlier that year when we'd made the top 12, we'd talked about how we both fancied exploring other avenues, and, having achieved that amazing result and performed all over the world and even been invited as one of eight couples to dance for Prince Mikasa, a member of the Japanese royal family, we felt like we had made it and achieved everything we needed to prove ourselves in the dance world. We just kept on believing we would be chosen as a couple – and, if we weren't chosen together, I assumed we'd support and help each other as we usually did.

The whole selection process took about five months and what's really strange is that I don't recall very much of the time between the first meeting and the screen test, except having this feeling that something exciting was about to happen.

A life-changing phone call

The phone call came early one morning – just before the trip to Hong Kong when Brendan would propose, and I would wonder why he'd done it. We'd been training late the night before and were still in bed. I was probably yawning when I picked up the phone and thought I was dreaming when I heard a voice say, 'We'd like to use both you and Brendan on the show.' But I wasn't dreaming. It really was the producers. When I told Brendan, still hardly believing it myself, we both leapt out of bed, cheering and jumping up and down like a couple of kids on Christmas morning when Santa's brought them everything on their list.

I was so excited that they'd taken both of us on. We were to be two of the original dancers on *Strictly Come Dancing* ... Wow!

CHAPTER 12
STRICTLY DESTINY

We'd done it! We were in! Our *Strictly* journey was about to begin ... and little did I know how much our lives were about to change. Brendan and I were equally excited, but I was, still am, intrigued by the fact that I was the one who had pushed for us to do the show. That's something that has always made me think that I could never blame anyone else for what happened later. I was the one who wanted to do the show after all. Maybe it was fate pushing me along. Who knows? But it reinforced something that has become a motto for me, a phrase I coined myself: 'Look inside for answers instead of outside for blame.'

I was thinking about how happy I was and how well our life was going. I couldn't remember the last time I'd cried – and I had cried lots when we hardly had two pennies to rub together and things were tougher than tough for us, but all that was about to change.

For the show, each professional dancer was paired with a celebrity who we had to train to bring them up to a standard where they could compete with their partner against the others. In that first season the big names included the opera singer Lesley Garrett, who danced with Anton du Beke; the actress Claire Sweeney, who was partnered by John Byrnes; and Christopher Parker, the actor and television presenter, who was paired with Hanna Karttunen.

We were all called to separate, secret meetings where we were introduced to our respective partners. It was no easy feat for the production team to keep the names out of the press until we had all met. All the celebs were given code names and we were only told our partners' real names when we were about to meet them. Brendan met his – a well-known and glamorous TV newsreader – a couple of days before I was introduced to mine.

He was over the moon at having been paired with her. It's no understatement to say that he literally skipped through the door when he came home that day, and to be honest that was the moment I lost the Brendan I thought I knew so well.

We normally shared every thought, every idea, every little thing, but suddenly it was as if his thoughts were elsewhere, and after that day I felt that he was distant and never really with me again. Usually I could read his every thought like a book, but that book was now closing. I had this terrible foreboding that something awful was about to happen. My heart was racing with anxiety and heavy with sadness at the same time.

I knew – I could sense – that he was on a mission to win the *Strictly* trophy at any cost. He was desperate to become famous and to prove something, not just to himself, but to his family and everyone else back in New Zealand, too.

I tried to talk to him, to find out what was going through his mind, but he'd lost interest in talking to me. He was more than happy, though, to get up in the morning to watch her reading the morning news!

My partner was the kind and fatherly TV presenter David Dickinson, but it was with a heavy heart that I met him. David lived 200 miles out of London and as I had to go there to teach him, it meant leaving Brendan in town to train and – I was sure – to flirt with his partner.

It was the first time we had worked apart for eight years, and we soon realized that we needed separate phones and email addresses. We had to leave the protected bubble that had sheltered us for all these years and join the real world.

I know it's irrelevant to my story, but to this day I have no idea whether it was Brendan's partner's fame and celebrity status that swept him away, or if he really did feel a strong connection with her. I'm guessing that it was probably a bit of both. What I do know though is that to me it felt as if the fact that we'd just got engaged meant nothing to either of them for the entire run of the show. The only thing that seemed to matter to them was the time they spent together, perfecting their Saturday performances. What was really hurtful was not just that Brendan appeared to have forgotten that he was engaged, the entire nation seemed to have forgotten that as well! It felt to me that everyone was buying into how lovely he and his *Strictly* partner were together and how much chemistry there was between them. I was so hurt that even now I can't find the words to describe the pain. And it wasn't made any easier that it was not just something private to Brendan and me, everyone else was reading about it in the papers.

Later, I received letters of support from fans of the show who wrote to say how much they felt for me. But when you're hurting as much as I was, you think that you are the only one in the world who has ever felt so devastated and that no one is on your side.

Angry words

Over the next few months we argued a lot and exchanged many angry and very hurtful words. I wanted – needed – to know why things were different and why we weren't spending any time together. I had to try to understand what was going on. But the only thing my questions led to was yet another fight. We even argued about arguing! All the time I could feel him slipping away from me. It was as if the tide was dragging him out to sea and I could no longer keep hold of his hand.

It felt like my best friend had literally disappeared in a day. I had no one close enough to turn to, and as my family was in Denmark, I had nowhere to go. If I'd opened my heart to any of our dancer friends, word would probably have spread like wildfire that my relationship with Brendan was on the rocks. Professional ballroom dancing is a hugely competitive sport and if I had tried to talk to anyone in the business, even the nicest ones would probably have thought, 'Another one down!' Harsh, maybe, but true of most if not all competitive situations.

Feeling sadder and lonelier than I ever had in my entire life, I had no choice but to put a smile on my face and get on with the training – with thoughts of Brendan and his partner always there at the back of my mind.

Training for *Strictly*

We practised with our celebrities for about a month before the first live show, something that meant spending most of the day together. A camera crew filmed our entire practice session – even if it took six hours – so our days were punctuated with coffee breaks, the occasional rest and the odd gentle disagreement. Sometimes, depending on the dance we were practising, we'd be filming in a salsa club or at a tea dance. All the footage was cut and edited, to be shown before our Saturday night performance. These 'highlights' were a way for the audience to get to know us – and hopefully to encourage them to give us their vote.

When we're training with our professional dancing partners, we're used to dancing closer than close, rubbing our bodies up and down each other for hours on end. Frankly, I never, ever consider this as being sensual or sexual. To professionals, dancing is an art and a sport, something we think of in very technical terms. The female is usually more concerned about how her arms, toes and legs are stretched and pulled than the way her partner is running his hand up and down her sides. The man will be worried about the timing of the step and what to lead next. It's mostly an act and it's about as sensual as swinging a golf club. But it's probably a different story for our amateur partners. They're not at all used to that body contact and when they're dancing with a professional whose wriggling his or her body against theirs, it can suddenly look much more suggestive than it really is.

You're doing this for hours on end, so it obviously helps if you get along with your partner and you get the amazing feeling that happens once in a while when two bodies manage to dance together in perfect harmony and synchronicity. I think perhaps that this is where some of the celebs get carried away, confused even, and when they're feeling sensual, happy and uplifted they let their emotions get the better of them. I'm sure you can imagine from the close relationship Brendan and I had, that when training and creating a performance together, you build an extremely strong bond in an extremely short time, and this can send out the wrong signals to someone who has probably only ever experienced this kind of bond with a lover.

The show must go on

15 May, 2004. A date I will never forget. The first night of the show. I've been putting off writing this part of the book for a very long time. It's difficult to put down on paper (well, a computer screen) what was to become the hardest time of my life. Having to remember what happened next will be an emotional journey of the toughest kind.

I know no one died, but I was about to hit rock bottom, have my heart broken and see my world turn upside down and inside out in the tap of a tango dancer's heel. And it was all going to happen in the glare of publicity. It was embarrassing. It was hurtful. And it came out of nowhere.

I know I'm not alone. I'm sure most of you will have been there at some point in your life. Heartache, grief or trauma of any kind all bring with them the same emotions – anger, sadness, hurt, guilt and fear.

You may agree with me then that the only positive thing when you hit rock bottom is that there's only one way to go. Up!

So, I'm sitting here thinking, 'Where do I begin? How do I tell this part of my story? How do I make you understand all my pain, while at the same time letting you know that everything will be OK in the end?'

The only positive thing when you hit rock bottom is that there's only one way to go. Up!

So ... 15 May, 2004. The first night of the show – the show I had pushed so hard to be on and had been so excited about from the outset.

It should have been so special, so exhilarating. Instead, it was a night full of sadness as I watched my fiancé slip even further away from me.

A few days earlier he'd surprised me by saying that he didn't want to share a changing room with me at the television studios. We'd always shared everything before, so why not now? Why was he suddenly making an issue of something that up till then I'd taken for granted? If proof were needed that things had changed between us, I had it.

Without discussing it with me, he simply said he'd prefer to be on his own while he was preparing for the show. Now, if he'd said this eight years earlier when our lives were not so intertwined and I was still very independent, it wouldn't have been a problem. But normally he'd been the one pushing to spend every moment together, so for him to say out of the blue that he wanted to be alone was completely out of character and a total shock for me. It fuelled my suspicion that his mind was on something other than us.

If I was hurt then, I was even more hurt on the first night of the show. We were about to go live. Everyone was dressed in the stunning gowns and suits that specialist dress designers had made for us. The theme tune was playing and we were all wishing each other good luck. The atmosphere was electric, as if everybody knew that we were about to take part in something very special. Most of us were lined up to make our entrance down the big flight of stairs that led to the dance floor when I saw that Brendan and his partner were still backstage below the stairs I was standing on. As I looked down, Brendan looked up, and when our eyes met he pulled his partner behind the curtain, and as he was leaning toward her, I knew that he was going to give her a good luck kiss. It wasn't just the kiss, it was the secrecy, the fact that he'd pulled her behind the curtain that made it feel as if someone had plunged a dagger through my heart.

I felt like crying, but what could I do? I was a professional dancer, and in two minutes our show was going out live to the UK for the first time.

Inside, I was hurting so much from the shock and the sadness, but all I could think of was, 'The show must go on.' So with me masking the pain behind my brightest show-business smile, David and I made our entrance.

All the time I was dancing with David that night I was crying inside. I'm a straightforward person and have always worn my heart on my sleeve. I believe that it's important to be honest even if it means confronting an uncomfortable situation. I like to clear the air and hate brushing things under the carpet. But that night I had to smile and dance as if all was right with my world, even though I believe bottled-up emotion to be toxic. I was desperate to let it out and scream aloud, 'Why are you doing these things? Why are you ruining everything we have fought for?'

Poor David forgot just about every step I'd taught him. I had to try to camouflage for him by moving around him as if I was dancing on air, which would have been extremely hard in normal circumstances: with my heart breaking inside me, it was nearly impossible, but I had to carry on and do it.

'Where's your fiancé?'

Meanwhile Brendan and his newsreader quickly became the nation's favourites, and please believe me when I say that I was genuinely thrilled for him. It's the honest truth. As ever, I wanted to offer him my help and support. I was desperate for us to be there for each other. When we got home that first night, we had yet another argument, with me demanding to know why he couldn't just give her a good luck kiss in front of me and Brendan brushing my moans aside, saying it made him feel awkward, that he was trying to get her to focus and calm her nerves. I wasn't reassured, but I had to try to be rational. After all, I had no actual evidence that he had in fact kissed her – maybe it was just my imagination running away with me. But I couldn't understand why he had to be so secretive.

I thought it would help if I met her properly, away from the studio, so over the next few weeks I asked Brendan several times if he would like to bring her home for dinner. That way I could get to know her and we could all be friends. I also asked him if I could help with their choreography and styling, something that I would normally have done as we did everything together.

Not this time, though: he said that it wasn't appropriate. And then he told me that he was going to 'pop over' to her house to help with her hair!

Help with her hair! That was strictly not necessary. We had a great team to do that for us on show days. I just thought that it was a ridiculous excuse for them to meet up.

'Can't I come, too?" I asked.

'Not appropriate!' he said again.

We'd been a couple for eight years and all that time we'd done everything together, but now when people asked me at the studio on show days, 'Where's your fiancé?' I didn't have a clue, and I was humiliated to have to admit it.

One day, the make-up artist who'd done Brendan and me for three weeks said, 'Oh, wow! I didn't know you were together let alone engaged.'

No wonder the alarm bells in my head were ringing louder and louder. All I wanted was to wake up and find that it had all been a nightmare: that everything would go back to how it used to be between us.

But that never happened.

CHAPTER 13
HOW DID IT ALL GO WRONG?

'If you are going through hell, keep going.'

(Author unknown)

Since turning professional, our fortunes had turned around. After years of scrimping and saving, we were now financially stable, well able to start treating ourselves to luxury brands when the fancy took us. New sunglasses? Gucci. New luggage? Mulberry. (And you can imagine how satisfying that was!)

We had even bought ourselves a flat – a newly built penthouse flat in Wallington, Surrey, with two floors, three bedrooms, three bathrooms, a huge lounge, dining space and kitchen. So much space. Brendan and I had gone through so much stress and hard work to get to this point in our lives. It had been a long journey. But now, as I sat there, alone in our brand-new apartment, close to tears, I asked myself over and over again, 'How did it all go so wrong?' and I realized the true meaning of that old saying: 'Money won't buy you happiness.' Now every time I spoke to Brendan it seemed to provoke a yet another argument. Often I'd be 200 miles away, training, and every time he said he was just off to meet his *Strictly* partner and her friends it broke my heart. Once he even said they'd just called his mum in New Zealand.

They'd just called his mum in New Zealand. 'Why?' I thought. 'Why on earth would you need to call his mum so she could speak to *her*?

Another time when all the dancers had been invited to a party and I was so excited about going with Brendan, he told me he was going with his celebrity dance partner instead! When I asked him why, he said they'd done so well in the competition that week, 'we wanted to celebrate our success together.' He was going with her and expected me to go on my own. I just couldn't make any sense of it. It was as if he'd slapped me on the face and expected me to say that I hope he hadn't hurt his hand!

Humiliated

I didn't want to involve my family as I knew how worried they'd be. And anyway, I was still hoping that we would manage to sort everything out ourselves.

But it was difficult to keep it a secret from my Mor as we are very close – always have been and always will be. We spoke every day, and no matter how hard I tried to hide it on the phone, she could tell something was up. Perhaps both she and my Far had detected the sadness in my voice. I don't know, I just know that they knew that I wasn't doing very well, and they decided to come over to watch one of the early shows live.

It should have been one of my proudest moments, having my parents sitting in the front row of the studio theatre. Instead I was filled with shame and humiliation. Why? Because, of all the shows to chose to do it, Brendan chose that particular one to congratulate his partner for their performance by kissing her on the lips. Right in front of the audience, and right in front of *my* parents and *his* future parents-in-law – he was kissing the woman who I now thought of as my arch-rival for his love.

My heart was lurching and I felt sick, desperately hoping that my parents hadn't seen it. I knew it would hurt them to see Brendan doing something that they knew would upset me. But they did see it – and so did everyone watching, including journalists. I could almost see them sitting at their computers writing articles about the oodles of obvious chemistry between Brendan and his partner. Maybe I was overreacting. Maybe it was 'just a kiss', just a 'well-done' gesture. But I couldn't stop asking myself if it was more than that.

The sixth season of *Strictly* that I was in held some very proud moments, but I never felt the need to kiss any of my partners on the lips, not even when Tom Chambers and I won it.

What made it worse was that it was totally out of character for Brendan to behave like that. I was seeing him with new eyes and thinking, 'Who is this guy?'

And then I had to suffer the mortification of my parents bringing it up after the show – saying what I was thinking, 'That seemed rather unnecessary …'

At rock bottom emotionally

And that's when it all caught up with me. It was just like the time when Mor asked if I was happy when I was 18 and in Copenhagen, living with Klavs's family. I broke down and sobbed and sobbed and sobbed. I had hit my emotional rock bottom – I have never felt so low in my entire life. I felt humiliated, confused and hurt to my very core.

I couldn't believe things were going to end like this – we'd been so close for so long that I couldn't accept this was the beginning of the end between us. I was still desperate to salvage what we'd had, because it had meant the world to me.

But every time I tried to get Brendan to open up, we got nowhere. He'd just repeat the same old words: 'I can't deal with this until the show's over.'

Who knows what he was thinking, I certainly didn't. Maybe he really was just focused on winning the trophy, confused, caught up in the whole thing and enjoying the limelight, thinking that I should just give him time, step aside and wait for me to get my head round what he was going through.

I couldn't. I was so hurt; I needed him to tell me that everything would be OK again.

I had certainly never known jealousy like this before – but then nor had I ever had to contend with watching my boyfriend – no, not my boyfriend, my fiancé – spending all his time with another woman, and what's more a woman he appeared to adore!

What now?

I was knocked out of the competition in week three, but the Open British Championships in Blackpool were around the corner, and we'd always planned to go back and compete there together. After all, that was our world and the place where we'd created our careers, got our next engagements and our bread-and-butter jobs. I assumed that although we were doing the show we'd still be going back to compete, and that we'd put on a united front and show the dance world that we weren't turning our back on it just because of a TV show.

But now Brendan had suddenly lost interest. It's hard to explain how his character, how everything that motivated him, seemed to have changed. He would always have been pushing to do the Open British: not to do it would have been unthinkable to him.

It was with something of a chill that I remembered the dancer who'd stood up at that first pre-*Strictly* meeting, and said that if the dancers on the show became celebrities it would make it difficult for them to return to their normal lives. 'What happens then?' she'd asked.

'What happens now?' I was asking myself.

Nobody thought that would happen – but it had. And it had happened to Brendan. Now, instead of honouring our commitment to each other and our career as a couple, he wanted to stay in London to practise with his celebrity partner – because, unlike me and the lovely David Dickinson, they were still in with a chance.

It seemed bizarre to me for him to place so much importance on the show though. At this point we had no idea how it would progress. It could have been a one-off, so I was far more concerned about keeping our other jobs and contacts happy so that we had work to keep us going after *Strictly Come Dancing* had finished.

Bye bye, Brendan

I begged him to discuss things with me and yes, I admit it, my needy behaviour was coming out in all its glory – not something I'm proud of. But I really wanted for us to sit down and talk about our relationship and what to do about Blackpool. I simply couldn't take it any longer. I was falling apart.

I didn't feel like I could talk to anyone who wasn't a friend of both of us or involved with the dance world in some way. But I couldn't cope any longer. Not knowing where I stood with my partner – whether I even still had a partner, not just on the dance floor but as a lover. Our careers, our lives, were intertwined.

I didn't want to give in and admit we were no longer working as a team. I simply wouldn't admit or accept that the strong bond we'd had no longer seemed to exist. I felt totally and utterly defeated. My life was in turmoil and I was in bits, I just wanted to curl up in a ball and cry.

I lost my appetite and I just felt totally stressed out. But even so, I put on my show-business smile and headed north for Blackpool on my own. Brendan had agreed to come up and watch the competition later on in the week, but he wouldn't compete. He preferred to stay on in London and train for *Strictly*. Hoping that he would give me a call to say he'd changed his mind and that he would come up earlier after all, I went along with it.

Before I went to Blackpool, I made one more attempt to fix things over one last conversation in our spanking new penthouse living room. I told him I felt so low I thought I was close to having a complete breakdown. I may as well have been talking to a brick wall. 'We can't have this conversation until the show's over,' he said.

I took a deep breath. 'If we can't talk about this in Blackpool at the latest, then I can't see what else I can do but to walk out the door and never come back.'

I couldn't live in this limbo. I was desperate for him to say, 'No don't go! Let's sit down and talk it through.' I so, so wanted to hear those words, because they would have been the balm I needed to soothe my wounded heart. But he didn't say anything – just that he couldn't deal with this now.

I knew in myself though that once I walked out the door it would be finished. As far as I'm concerned, when something is over, it's over. It's time to move on, however hard that may be.

Yet again, he said he couldn't take any decisions about how he felt and that he wanted to wait until the show had finished. I told him that I felt so broken, sad and upset that I just couldn't do it anymore and that what he was saying wasn't good enough for me. I needed him to cool things with his dance partner, although of course I knew they'd have to finish the competition together. I still wanted him to win. I just didn't want us to throw away everything we had worked for.

Even at that point, I still thought that we stood a chance if he dealt with it and made me part of his journey again – just like he always had. He asked me to bear with him until the series came to an end, when he would talk about things and let me know how he felt. But I couldn't even watch *Strictly* anymore, it was too painful. And when we had to go on a sister talk show with Justin Lee Collins and all play happy families, I felt nauseated.

Media frenzy

The press went crazy with rumours after the first live show and not long after I had to move out of our apartment. But before I did, journalists were constantly buzzing the entryphone, trying to get me to comment on stories about us in the papers. They knew I was in the flat – why else would they be pressing that blasted buzzer – but even so, one paper had it that I had *already* moved out because of the chemistry between Brendan and his partner, and all the rumours of an affair between them. It was so hurtful. I hadn't moved out at all! I was still there – curled up and crying in the corner of the couch, feeling so alone.

They managed to get into the building and started to push notes under the door, asking me to sell them my side of the story. They even tried to call my parents in Denmark for their comments.

I had no idea what they expected me to say. But, whatever it was, I didn't want to say it! So I called a friend and asked her to pick me up. I just needed to get out of there. I wasn't interested in talking to anyone about what was going on. How could I? I didn't even know what was going on myself!

That evening my lovely friend took me for a Chinese meal with some of her friends to try and cheer me up, but it didn't really work because, soon after we got to the restaurant, my phone started ringing. It was Brendan, phoning with his celeb dance partner, from a cab they were sharing after their *Strictly* practice.

He sounded agitated. He knew the press was on my back, but I knew it wasn't my back that he wanted to protect. It was his and hers. 'We think it's best if you don't talk to the newspapers about all this,' he said.

'*We think it's best!*' Suddenly they were the couple and I was the outsider who had to keep her mouth shut. What about Brendan and I sitting down and trying to discuss what the press was doing to *us*? Where was Brendan's loyalty to *me*? He was my best friend, the only person in the world I could turn to. Now I felt as if he had turned on me, and it was as if he'd pulled my heart out and stamped on it.

All I knew was that I had to get away. So I went home to Denmark, leaving Brendan to get on with the show until the final night when we were all expected to be there. Well, to be fair, it was no surprise when Brendan and his partner won. I'm enough of a professional to know that they were good. But as I stood there, congratulating them, it felt as if I was talking to someone I didn't know, let alone the man I'd shared my life with and had been due to marry!

I was really proud of his achievement but so deeply hurt I could hardly hold myself together. All the other contestants were really supportive and I tried to play it cool to make it less awkward for everybody else. I think I managed it.

Big girls do cry

After that, I went straight back to Denmark, away from it all. Hanging out in my sister's house gave me the peace and calm to confront the pain. The grief I felt was, I later understood, no different from the grief I felt when we lost our dog Besy, when I was 13. I'd wept uncontrollably then; I wept uncontrollably now.

I kept on telling myself to stop feeling so sad when there were so many people around the world going through far worse things. There were wars going on. What's a little heartache? What right had I to be this upset? But Jeanet said, 'Sis, it's OK to be sad and cry. Everything is relative, and you need to get this out of your system.'

It was as if she gave me permission to cry, to be sad, to grieve for my loss, and I will always love her for that. She wasn't just my sister, she was an amazing friend through that time. She never judged me. Never judged my relationship. And never questioned the situation I was in. She just let me figure it all out in my own time, while being there for me.

Over the summer there would be many chances for Brendan to come to see me and try to put things right; but he never did. I can't say how I would have reacted if he had, or even if it would have been too late. It's irrelevant now. But the bottom line is that he decided to stay in the UK to do a DVD with his celebrity partner that summer instead.

'I'm not really bothered!'

For years Brendan and I had been really keen to be considered good enough to represent England in the World Championship. And guess what! While I was staying with my sister in Copenhagen after the *Strictly* final, that invitation finally came through. Not just that. We were also asked to perform at the *Night of 100 Stars*, one of the most glamorous and prestigious evenings in the ballroom world. I called Brendan to discuss it, imagining he'd still want to go ahead, even if only as professional partners. It was, after all, something we'd dreamed of for so long. His answer? 'I'm not really bothered!' I was shocked and numb at the same time. I hung up the phone and realized that this was it. We really were through. Then I took the book containing the business cards from all our contacts around the world and threw it in the bin. I knew I would be starting over, and this time I'd be alone. I had lost my partner, my home and my career, all in one fell swoop. I felt as if the rug into which my entire life had been woven had been pulled from beneath my feet.

The only way is up

While I was trying to pull myself together back in Copenhagen, I thought that a visit to the gym would boost my spirits. But as I stood on the StairMaster – a piece of equipment I normally enjoyed using – I found I had no strength at all, not even for one step. This is when I knew I really was at the lowest I had ever been. I was emotionally and physically drained! I had to jump off the machine and just go home.

Back at Jeanet's house I realized that if I was that down (and believe me I was that down) there was only one way to go and that was up. I had to dig deep but eventually something clicked inside me. I found an inner strength I didn't even know I had. It was a turning point, and, however sad I was, I decided then and there that each day I would walk outside in the fresh air, taking one step at a time to build up my strength until I was running a good 20 minutes. Bearing in mind that I'd always hated running, this was definitely a new beginning. Every step I took I saw as being one more step away from that sad situation with Brendan, and one step closer to finding myself and my confidence again.

I now love walking and running and find it extremely empowering. It's grounding – almost meditative – and it will always be one of my favourite ways to get a perspective on things, especially if I'm upset and want to get rid of all the negative energy that creates.

Gaining strength

Rock bottom is a sad and lonely place to be. Being there may make you feel broken, that doesn't mean to say it's a hopeless place to be. Knowing now that you really are as low as you can go, means you can now start working your way up again.

In my case, having parted from my dance partner, business partner and lover, I started thinking about how I would put the pieces back together again and also how I would create a career for myself. I find it so fascinating that it sometimes takes something so sudden, explosive and surprising to wake us up from the trance in which we sometimes live, and give us a chance to take a proper good look at ourselves.

I know a lot of people are quick to blame everyone and everything around them, and I think somewhere in my grieving period I had a moment of self pity when I asked Brendan how he could do this to me. That was a real 'poor me' moment! But I started reading a lot of motivational books and I listened to hypnosis CDs from Anthony Robbins and Paul McKenna to build up my shattered confidence, and *I found an inner strength I didn't even know I had* it wasn't too long before I pulled myself out of 'Poor Me City'. Trust me, this is not a place to linger if you want to find true happiness within. I used to wake up every day and wonder if I would ever feel truly happy again. I really couldn't imagine how it used to feel or how long it would take for me to see the light at the end of the tunnel – but I now know that when we are in the 'poor me' state of mind we are not attractive to ourselves or the world around us. If you don't believe me, just think of the times you have been hanging out with friends who have pulled a 'poor me'. How they have complained about this and that, and how you yearned to say, 'Come on! Take a look at yourself!' There are lots of things you can do for yourself, but sitting and complaining about what everyone else is doing wrong is not going to improve your situation at all. In fact you will probably just attract even more bad news into your life. Remember how earlier I spoke about how the law of attraction works? When we notice 'poor me' popping up, it's a sign that it's time to take action.

LEARN TO SAY 'YES!'

I took inspiration from a great improv acting exercise called 'Yes let's' and you can adopt this simple and effective attitude right now.

When I was going through my 'poor me' stage after my break with Brendan, all I wanted to do was to hide and lick my wounds, but after wallowing in self pity for a while, I told myself it was time to pull myself together.

I think the final push was when I had gone on holiday with my family to help cheer myself up and cried for most of it. Not only was I heartbroken, but I also had come down with tonsillitis because of all of the stress. I remember crying and telling Mor that she seriously didn't understand how low I was, when clearly she did. I know now that anyone who's been heartbroken or bereaved would understand what I was going through, but at the time I thought, like most people do, that no one could possibly understand the pain I was in.

Anyway, when I got home from holiday I thought, 'Enough of this self pity already, pull yourself together, girl.' I think I'd read a book called *Yes Man* and it had inspired me to start saying, 'Yes!'

When friends invited me out I started saying, 'Yes!'

When colleagues suggested an outing to a band or event that sounded random to me I said, 'Yes!'

If a friend asked me to a dinner party full of strangers I said, 'Yes!'

I even challenged myself to go out and have dinner on my own in restaurants. The alternative was to sit at home alone and feel sad about everything that had gone wrong.

When you come out of a relationship you often think that you can't do something on your own and that all your friends are couples, so you'll never meet anyone again. I thought that way too for some time, but then I thought, 'Says who?'

If you are bored of sitting at home feeling sorry for yourself, then start getting involved in the things around you. When somebody invites you along to something say, 'Yes!' even if at first you think that's not really your kind of thing. Saying, 'Yes!' has led me to meeting so many interesting people and making new friends, too, and most important of all it got me out of the self-pity bubble and back on the track toward happiness.

This attitude is one that I ask many of my business clients to adopt too. It's a great way to keep creativity going in the office and when someone comes up with an idea it's much more positive to give them a 'Yes!' and then add to it, instead of shooting them down with a 'No!'

Yes!' keeps the creative juices flowing.

CHAPTER 14
NO GOING BACK

After a summer trying to come to terms with my heartache, I returned to England to the news that (a) there was to be a second season of *Strictly Come Dancing* and I had been invited back and (b) ... Brendan had also been asked to return.

Not only that. So had she! His celebrity partner was going to stand in for Tess Daley who was to be on maternity leave for the first few shows.

Say *yes* and not only would I have to work alongside Brendan again, but I'd also have to face his celeb partner who'd be interviewing me live on air week after week. I couldn't imagine a more cringe-worthy situation to be in. I felt as if I was being asked to act in a farce starring my work and my love life. But, say *no*, and I'd have to throw away this fantastic job on TV, doing the thing I felt like I'd been put on earth to do.

The words 'emotional' and 'turmoil' don't come within a mile of describing how I felt as I tried to reach a decision.

Even though I'd been in Denmark and missed a lot of the stuff in the papers, I knew there'd been all that gossip and that most other people had read it. If I came back, I'd have to be so cautious with the press. I knew that interviews around the show would be inevitable, they're part of the job, and I knew that some reporters would try to lure me into talking about the Brendan situation. The very thought of that made me feel sick.

Should I stay or should I go?

Half of me wished I could just walk away from my break-up the way most people do: close the door on it and not open it again until my heart was whole again. But the other half wanted to carry on. *Strictly* is the most wonderful journey and with the words of the philosopher Friedrich Nietzsche in mind – 'What doesn't kill you makes you stronger' – I decided it was a journey I had to make again.

I'd been in it since the beginning and seen it grow from an idea floated at Blackpool to a top-of-the-ratings, Saturday night success. Despite what had happened, I still felt a part of the *Strictly* family. To say it was a difficult decision is something of an understatement, but after a lot of heart-searching I agreed

> '*What doesn't kill you makes you stronger*'
> FRIEDRICH NIETZSCHE

to go back, and out came my brave, smiling face as I pretended that all was right in my world, when only I knew that, inside, it definitely wasn't. But I was certain about one thing: I was not going to bring 'poor me' to work.

DO YOU EVER BRING 'POOR ME' TO WORK? TRY THIS …

1. Ask yourself now if feeling sorry for yourself is going to help you move forward or could you now consider that there may be another way.

2. Decide now to refuse to let that 'poor me' state of mind take over and you'll notice you start seeing, feeling and hearing things differently, putting them in a new perspective.

3. With that in mind, now finish this sentence: 'I feel sorry for myself because …' writing down your answer helps put the

---

situation into perspective. Realising what we don't want helps us realise what we do want.

4. Now shift your focus from a place of lack of love, which the 'poor me' attitude is, to a new one with an abundance of 'happy me'. Finish the sentence: 'I feel good about myself when I ...' again writing down your answer.

5. Notice what you've written, see what makes you happy, and start focusing on all the positive things in your life by finishing this sentence: 'In my life I am grateful for ...' writing as many things as you can think of, and you will find that the 'poor me' place will start to disappear and will no longer seem so attractive to you. When you have reached this stage you will start to focus on what makes you happy.

Emotional roller coaster

Now, I am by no means saying that we shouldn't acknowledge how we are feeling if we are angry, hurt or sad. What I am saying is that we should not dwell on them. I refused to let my personal feelings get in the way of my work. Having grown up in show business, I knew all too well the meaning of the words, 'the show must go on' and I had no choice but to make them my mantra for the second season.

When I was shattered after Brendan, I could have spent years feeling sorry for my broken heart and myself. I could have blamed the world and not taken any responsibility for what had happened. But doing that would have made me feel like I was being tossed around in a giant emotional roller coaster. Instead, I decided to take control of the one thing I could control: my own thoughts. I could be in charge of how I felt, where I put my focus and what I thought about. I could also control the words I used to describe my situation and how I was going to heal and learn from this experience in order to grow. I kept on reading those feel-good books I'd got into when I was in Denmark staying with Jeanet, and listening to positive-thinking and, as I said earlier, even hypnotherapy CDs. I know there are people who scoff at things like that. All I can say is they helped me to take charge of my own life and put me in a place where I'm happy to be.

There are times in all our lives when we try to control situations that are outside of ourselves. This is a complete waste of energy as there is no way we can change how others feel, act and behave. But what we can control is how *we* react to them.

Not long after I broke up with Brendan, someone told me it would probably take me three years to heal fully. I'd like to say they were wrong, but in fact they were right. It was a big old journey of inward discovery and healing that I embarked on, but embark on it I did.

And while I was on the journey, I kept thinking of what had become one of my favourite quotes: 'People of accomplishment rarely sat back and let things happen to them. They went out and happened to things.' –Leonardo da Vinci

Maybe what I've just said is making you think that this would be a good time to stop and ask yourself whether you are taking responsibility for your journey: whether you are in charge and are truly the designated driver of the car taking you through your life.

Cause and effect

If you are making yourself the victim, constantly banging on about how bad things happen to you, and how you didn't do this, that and the next thing because of something someone else did or said ... if you are doing all this then, in neurolinguistic programming (NLP), you are on the effect side rather than the cause side of things.

Let me explain the simple principle of what is described in NLP as being on the cause and effect side of a situation. Take your work. Would you say that you are in control of your actions there? Do you take responsibility for them? Or do you blame other people for the things that happen to you and pull a 'poor me'?

If you want to do better at something at work, do you make it happen – or do you let people around you determine how you are doing and let them decide whether it's going to happen or not?

If I ask you to imagine you're in a car, what is your first thought? Are you the driver, or the passenger? If you are the driver then you have put yourself on the cause side of things and you are in control of your own destiny. If you are the passenger you have put someone else in charge and you're on the effect side.

TRY THIS ...

Start by writing down a situation that is bothering you right now, and then consider this statement: 'We are the authors of our own life stories.' In other words, the thoughts that we think, and the words that we speak, have an impact on how our lives pan out.

- If you agree with that, then you are on the cause side, you're on the right track. If you disagree, then this exercise may help you to think about things in a new and positive way.
- Look back at the situation you wrote down and now describe next to it why it's bothering you. Use as few or many words as you like.
- When you've done that, take a look at how you have described the situation, and especially the words you used. Were you blaming everyone else or did you take responsibility, too?
- An example of blaming, which means you being the victim, the 'poor me', could be that your boss never listens to you when you speak to her. She expects too much of you at

work and you simply haven't got enough hours in the day to complete your workload. She makes you feel like you're slow and not up to the job and that's what makes you sad.

- Or it could be something in your private life. Maybe your boyfriend (or girlfriend) is making you feel low and not good enough about yourself. It could be that when he suggests you go out for a run or go to the gym you immediately think he is saying you are not good enough as you are.

- Now, here's the thing. No one can make you feel like that if you don't want them to. You are in charge of your own emotions and how you feel depends on you and only you. If you truly don't already love yourself and feel good enough all the time, I urge you to start now. We are all fabulous, beautiful human beings who can choose to love or not to love ourselves. So knowing that and believing it, why not choose to love yourself? Please give it a go. Everything looks so much brighter when we start loving ourselves.

Let's look at the office situation again but this time putting ourselves on the cause side, taking charge of our own situation, looking at what we can do if we take responsibility.

- So if your boss isn't listening to you, ask yourself how you can make him give you his attention. This is a pro-active approach to the issue that puts you in charge. Find out if he prefers to communicate via email, phone calls or in face-to-face meetings. Maybe you could ask if he has five minutes to talk through a couple of things you would like his opinion on? Most of our problems are based on a lack of communication and once we actually talk an issue through with the person we think we have an issue with, then it's usually easily clarified. Doing this is putting yourself in charge, showing that you're willing to work on improving a situation, and that's far more productive than spending your energy sitting feeling sorry for yourself and telling everyone else about your 'problem', which usually just seems to magnify it anyway. Putting yourself on the cause side could, of course, also lead you to another conclusion where you come to realize that your values and the values of the business you are working for don't match and you can then make plans accordingly, now that you have taken charge.

- Now let's look at that boyfriend (or girlfriend) problem. Could it be that in fact it's not him who's making you feel like that, maybe it's you who's feeling guilty about not exercising as much as you would like? Could it even be that you are not yet loving yourself enough and that's what's making you feel low? The only way you can fix this is by taking charge. Very often when someone speaks to us, we don't really hear what they're saying; we hear what we think they are saying. And if you're not feeling good about yourself, when he says, 'Do you want to go for a run?' you hear, 'You are unfit, not good enough and need to go for a run.' So sit down and plan how you can put more exercise into your schedule and next time he suggests a run you'll hear them for what they really mean: 'Want to hang out and exercise together?'

  If he really meant it as you heard it first time round and you already love and value yourself, then, putting yourself on the cause side, think about reconsidering your relationship; and if you decide not to end it, then at least ask him to respect and love you exactly how you are.

Breaking up is hard to do

After a break-up it's easy to lose your confidence and start querying whether you are 'good enough'. Often, when you're getting over a broken relationship you feel sad and depressed at work and rather than blame what's happened, you think it's your boss or colleagues who are making you feel like that. This is something you have to address sooner or later if you want to fully heal. If you ever find yourself in that situation you may want to try this – it helped me a lot. Ask yourself now what needs to happen for you to feel good enough all the time and to not be a 'victim'. It could be a simple thing like learning to set boundaries in your life, learning to say, 'No!' Most of us realize that it often starts with learning how to love ourselves and how to feel good enough inside and out all the time. It could be a situation long ago, maybe when we were children, that made us feel this way.

Whatever it is, you need to work out why you are not feeling good enough all the time or why you feel sad or disappointed with yourself constantly. What's extraordinary is that we almost always know the answers in our hearts and minds, if we just take the time to actually listen to the messages our bodies and minds send us we'd know that. Feeling good enough in ourselves is the foundation on which we can build everything else in our lives. Once you've learned that, happiness will flood into every aspect of your life, including your place of work.

This feeling of only feeling good enough sometimes or even never can appear in even the most successful of people at any time in their lives, as I have seen in many of my clients. It is a very common issue that we all have to work through at some stage or other and is often the root cause of most problems.

WRITE THIS DOWN

What needs to happen for me to start feeling good enough all the time?

Write down whatever answer comes to mind first and keep on writing until you have your solution in front of you. Writing it down will really help you to clear it from your mind and put it into perspective.

CHAPTER 15
RESCUE ME

So there we were again – back in the BBC studios in London's Shepherd's Bush, preparing to wow the UK with a second season.

It wasn't going to be easy for me but I was determined to give it my best shot and, even though my heart broke every time I saw Brendan, I thought I could hide my pain from the world.

And, guess what – I succeeded!

Only one person knew what I was going through, and that was Erin Boag, one of the *Strictly* dancers who'd been teamed with Martin Offiah in the first season and made it to the fifth round.

I'd picked up the phone one day when I was staying with my sister in Denmark and there was Erin. 'Hi, Babe,' she said. 'How are you?'

I tried to fob her off with a 'Fine! Thanks!' But Erin was too wise for that. 'OK,' she said, 'here's the deal. Obviously I know you're not really fine – but I want you to know that when you come back to the UK, and when you're ready to see people, I'll be there for you.'

I can't tell you how much that meant to me. I needed one friend on the show, someone who cared, even if I didn't want to talk about it.

You're probably wondering why on earth I'd agreed to go back to the show – but you will know by now that I believe that everything happens for a reason; that even when we make a 'wrong' choice, that choice is meant to be. I had chosen to be in the first season of *Strictly* – and ironically so, as Brendan had at first been reluctant. That choice had led to the break-up with my lover of eight years and fiancé of three months. But even in my darkest times I carried on believing that everything happens for a reason – I just wished I could see what the purpose of all this pain could possibly be.

And though it may seem that when I agreed to go back, I was just opening the wound and rubbing salt into it, this is when things started to turn around for me. Suddenly three new men flew into my life like angels to pick me up.

Angel number 1

The first was the dancer Ian Waite. We had known each other for years through the professional dance circuit, and not only was he a brilliant dancer but he was also fantastic fun to be with. We'd always been able to share a joke – even when we were trying to beat each other to win a trophy.

Well, talk about synchronicity – being in the right place at the right time – it turned out that Ian had just come back to the UK after several years based in Holland, and he, too, had just split from his dance partner.

Someone suggested that we two lost souls try out together, and, though I felt funny at first about dancing with someone who wasn't Brendan – after all, I'd thought Brendan and I would end our dance careers together – it took just a few steps with Ian to convince me otherwise. It felt so right that it was as if the universe was saying, 'There you go. This is all part of the big plan for your life.' And, with an inward sigh of relief, I realized I'd just caught my first glimpse of the light at the end of the tunnel.

Ten years on, Ian is still my dance partner and we have performed together all over the UK, appeared on *Strictly Come Dancing*, and made it to the top 12 in the International Championships.

Ian also came with an added bonus: he was gay. And, for the first time since Kenneth, I had a close and enduring relationship with my permanent dance partner that was not a romantic or sexual one.

Angel number 2

My next angel was the Olympic gold medallist Roger Black – my celebrity partner for the new *Strictly* season. He was eight years older than me and married to a wonderful woman called Jules, who I immediately made it my business to get to know.

We *Strictly* couples had to spend a ridiculous amount of time together and I found it was actually helpful to our dancing and our chances of success if we got on well with our partner's partner. I didn't want any other wife or girlfriend to suffer the way I had with Brendan, wondering what was happening when their partner was spending so much time with someone else. So, straight away, I asked to meet Roger's wife and set up involving her as much as possible in our preparations for the competition, so much so that I'd ring her and say, 'If Roger comes home grumpy then blame me – I've shouted at him 15 times today!' Getting someone 'onside' is, I have learned, vital in helping you to control a situation, and I wanted to make the situation Jules, Roger and I were in as happy a one as possible for all concerned.

Roger had found fame as an athlete and was now a superb and really inspiring motivational speaker. He and I shared many stories about the power of the mind. I especially remember how we both said that the first thing anyone ever asks us is, 'How many hours do you train?' It was one of those questions that drove us mad though, because we both knew that when it came to training it wasn't how much time you put in, but how well you used that time. Two hours of quality training were worth far more than five hours when your heart just wasn't in it. That's something most successful people can relate to.

Looking back at season two and all those conversations with Roger, I know he was significant in influencing my own later career as a public speaker, and when he took me to hear him give one of his talks I thought, 'Oh my God! This is what I want to do with my life.' I knew then that I was someone who wanted many careers – I wasn't destined just to be a dancer. I've said it before, I'll say it again: 'Thank you, Roger!'

Roger and I talked a lot about the power of the ego – and how we had to put our own egos aside when we worked as a team.

Often when we get upset about something it's actually just because our ego – the opinion we have of ourselves, our abilities and our sense of importance – is bruised or feels precious. Ego can take over when you start believing your own hype. Tell yourself often enough that you don't need others to help you succeed and your ego will come to the surface. It's important to recognize when this happens, as the ego can be more detrimental than you might imagine. It can hold you back and make you blinkered.

Here's an example of that. During season three of *Strictly*, we were suddenly asked if all the professionals could get together and create a group number. Up until this moment we had only ever performed as couples – never as an ensemble – so you can imagine the clash of egos that caused. Not only did we have to work together, we had to take it in turns to choreograph the routine, which meant, obviously, dancing to someone else's steps, not something we were used to doing. But after a week or two, our egos were put to one side and we all came to realize that we were stronger together, pooling our talents and skills to create something magical, something that filled us all with pride and something that brought us closer together as a group. I urge you to think about that the next time your ego gets in your way. Simply say to yourself, 'If I put my ego aside, how am I actually feeling about this situation? Could I in fact benefit and learn from this collaboration?'

Angel number 3
And then there was Fabio …

I was in no way ready to start a new relationship, and I was definitely not looking for one. I was broken and sore and needed to mend my heart before I did that. And then I met Fabio – a tall, dark and handsome Italian with a sexy accent and no connection whatsoever with the entertainment world ...

I was in 'keeping busy' mode when I met him. By day, when I wasn't working, I'd sit listening to Paul McKenna tapes to boost my confidence. By night, I'd go out with friends as much as I could, trying to keep my mind off my loss.

One night a Danish friend took me to a bar and in walked Fabio. After chatting for a bit, he asked if I'd like to meet for coffee some time. I thought it sounded nice and casual – so, one lunchtime we met up. And what I discovered was that although I was far from ready for a relationship of any kind, I was also far from ready to admit it. I was desperate to feel safe and loved again and in my ignorance I thought that was the way to heal. I've learned since then that trying to replace the man who broke your heart is not the same as healing a broken heart. But Fabio was unlike any man I had met before – he was so gentle and kind, yet very sophisticated, serious and Italian. They say that when you go into a new relationship often your new partner can be the total opposite of your last one. That was the case with Fabio. He worked in finance, which was so refreshing. It meant that we would talk about lots of different things and for the first time in ages my mind was opening to the world around me. I realized what a cocoon I'd been living in for all those years.

Entering into this, a new relationship made me feel very vulnerable, but over the next three years Fabio taught me how to trust, love and be independent again, and I taught him to believe in his ability, take chances and pursue his dreams, and encouraged him to go for a job he really wanted.

I genuinely have no doubt that we were sent into each other's lives to teach one another different things, and although our relationship did come to an end, we are still good friends.

I really do believe that the universe has always provided me with the right people at the right time in my life. Even if someone has been sent to challenge me, which is hugely annoying, frustrating and exhausting at the time, it has proved super-helpful in the long run. I think we are put in a similar position over and over again until we learn whatever lesson it is we need to learn. Whether it's to learn to love ourselves, feel good enough all the time, or – as in my case – to learn to respect ourselves and set boundaries. This is why it is so important, when we come out of a challenging situation, to ask ourselves, 'What do I need to learn from this experience?'

I had thought I'd learned to respect myself and set boundaries when I confronted my boss and walked out of that job in Denmark when I was 19. But then I'd been set the same challenge again when Brendan made me feel like s**t. Once again I'd been treated with no consideration for my feelings and once again I'd had to walk out in order to protect my self-respect.

Back in Copenhagen, nursing 'poor me' after Brendan, I'd taken myself off to see a psychic who'd left me with some wise words. She told me never to let the actions of others change who I am. She could see that I was someone who, when I loved, I loved with 100 per cent of my being: there was nothing half-hearted about my relationships. 'Don't let a broken heart change that,' she said. 'You *will* love again.'

They were such amazing words and so true to me – and I always remembered them when I found myself tempted to put up a protective barrier to stop myself from getting close to someone. Her words would come into my head again and I'd think: 'What's the worst thing that can happen?' Well, I knew that the worst thing would be that I'd be left with a broken heart and I'd think, 'Been there! Had the T-shirt! Binned it!' In other words, I'd survived. And then I'd jump in feet first and fall fully in love again, remembering yet again never to let the actions of others change who you are.

That psychic's words meant so much, because, yes, I am someone who gives everything. I wear my heart on my sleeve and I speak honestly about my feelings and if that means getting hurt then so be it, because when you love fully, I believe you are also loved fully in return, which is exactly why it is important not to enter into a new relationship with baggage as that is probably what you will meet, too. Sadly for Fabio, though, I was not yet ready to *fully* love 100 per cent when I met him. I was still too broken. I know that now. But I remember meeting the man I'm married to now, Kevin, and falling madly in love and having that moment where we both looked each other in the eyes and knew that this was it. It was as if we were saying to each other that if we give ourselves fully to this relationship we would be entering a very vulnerable place and opening ourselves up to the possibility of being very deeply hurt. But then we both agreed to take that risk, open our hearts, and give each other all we had to give – and it was the best feeling in the world.

LET YOURSELF LOVE

Remember Alfred, Lord Tennyson's words: 'Tis better to have loved and lost, than never to have loved at all.' There was a time in my life when I seriously queried this, but not any more. When you love fully it is the best feeling in the world.

Love lessons

Have you ever thought that when someone attacks you with words, it could be that they are feeling a lack of love? That perhaps it's not really a personal attack on you?

I'm not saying that this justifies their behaviour, but sometimes understanding what that person is dealing with helps bring the situation to a place where positive communication can take place and solutions can be created.

I am still proud that when I broke up with Brendan, I never turned bitter or went into blame mode. Yes, I was hurt and angry and I took 100 per cent responsibility for the part I'd played, too. I read in a lot of inspirational books that anger, hate and blame are only hurtful to yourself and can often manifest as some sort of disease within our bodies. This spurred me on to look for ways to get rid of the anger I had toward the situation and the people who had hurt me, rather than letting it fester.

TRY THIS

When I was healing my broken heart I came across this very helpful tool that I want to share with you. It's very simple: it entails writing a letter to the person who hurt you – lover, friend, colleague, family member whatever – but never sending it.

Whatever you need to get off your chest, get it all out in this letter. The good thing is that you can be completely honest as no one except you will ever read it. It's such a therapeutic experience. And it can even work when you write this letter to someone who has already passed away. (In fact, doing that is an excellent way of starting to come to terms with grief.) The point is that writing it down helps clear the anger from your mind. Use the letter to say all the things you want to tell them but can't, because in doing so you'd probably solve nothing and just cause bigger problems and pain: the other person may not be in the same place as you right now and they may see it differently to you. Once you have got it all off your chest, imagine you are sending the letter, but instead just rip it up and throw it in the bin. You should find this a very liberating experience.

By not actually sending this letter, you are not creating more hurt but you are releasing the anger, sadness, fear, guilt and hurt from yourself; getting rid of the feelings that are no longer serving you.

I call this the letter of forgiveness: you set the person free from you and you forgive them.

'But I don't want to forgive him!'

I have often heard clients say that, to which I reply, 'Forgiveness is not the same as agreeing with the actions of others. You don't have to agree with the way someone has treated you or condone their actions. But by forgiving them you are not holding onto resentment and anger. It doesn't serve you and does nothing except to make you bitter, and that's something that will hold you back and stop you from enjoying your life to the full.

It's totally OK to say, 'I forgive you but I don't agree with your actions.' This way you are now free to move on in your life. If you have some doubt about what I have just said, then please – not for my sake but for yours – ask yourself honestly right now, 'What do I achieve by holding onto this anger in my life?' And then, 'What will letting go of this anger add to my life?'

Some people ask why they shouldn't send a letter of forgiveness. Here's an example of why not. Say you are annoyed about your parents being controlling, how would it be helpful to send the letter to them? They are probably doing the best they can, and are not even aware

Never let the actions of others change who you are

of the fact that you see their behaviour as controlling. It's part of being a parent to want to do the best for their children. Perhaps what you see as control they see as love, even if their attitude upsets you. In some cases, their behaviour might well be controlling, but perhaps that's the only way they know how to behave.

Just understanding a situation like that helps to make it easier to handle. If you then write the letter it clears all those negative thoughts from your mind and it's more than likely that you will notice that although you never sent the letter, something in the universe has shifted and you will find that the next time you see that person, whether you want to or not, things are different. Maybe because you have cleared it from your mind, forgiven and accepted that they are trying their best.

If it's someone you don't have to see, then it's even easier. They will just disappear from your thoughts and all the resentment, hate and anger toward them will simply vanish along with them, leaving you free to carry on with a more healthy, loving attitude in life. Remember that we can never make anyone else change. Other people are out of our control. We can only ever change ourselves. Trying to change someone else is a waste of your time. If you wish for someone to improve their behaviour, the best thing I can suggest – however hard it is – is to lead by example. Remember the wonderful maxim often attributed to Mahatma Gandhi: 'Be the change you want to see in the world.' Be absolutely brilliant, be the change that others may follow, be the inspiration, but start by making that change within yourself.

After the letter exercise, I often use another one to make sure I have cut the emotional ties. This exercise can work with people you no longer want to associate with, but also with people who you do need to see again. It just helps to prevent them draining your energy and by personally taking the decision to cut the ties, you are not wasting valuable energy focusing on a problem situation – instead you can put that energy to better use healing yourself.

I always send the balloon away with love. Just because you don't get on with someone doesn't mean you don't want them to do well, heal and find happiness within, too. I really do believe in karma: what goes around comes around. A great rule of life I believe is to treat people how you would like to be treated.

THE BALLOON EXERCISE FOR CUTTING THE TIES

1. When you have five minutes to call your own, sit or lie down somewhere you feel relaxed.
2. Think about the person or situation you feel is draining your energy.
3. Now put that person or situation in a balloon that you imagine yourself holding.
4. Close your eyes and imagine yourself cutting or letting go of the string.
5. Now see the balloon float away into the distance until it's so small it has disappeared.
6. Notice how you feel as you watch the balloon float away into nothingness. You should feel energized, having let go of these feelings and emotions attached to that old situation or person. You can repeat this exercise again and again until the emotion is completely gone.

CHAPTER 16
LEARNING TO LOVE AGAIN

Fabio was good for me: not the heartbreak cure I'd imagined, but good for me anyway. And, although we were close, our relationship was an 'on–off' one, something that turned out to be another blessing in disguise – because, when our season three celebrity partners were announced, another angel flew into my life.

The TV chef James Martin came along at a time when I was seriously doubting that I'd ever meet anyone with whom I'd have the same chemistry – that mysterious magnetic attraction – I'd shared with Brendan. But the moment I met James, I recognized that invisible chemistry again. We hit it off straight away and became extremely close. We reached the semi-finals, but better than that, I learned so much from our friendship.

1. Brendan wasn't the only soul mate I'd ever have

James came into my life just as I was starting to emerge from my period of mourning for Brendan. I was still far from healed – but I could feel a small ray of hope starting to glow inside me; the hope that maybe one day I would be able to love fully again, just as that Danish psychic had promised. By reminding me of what it was like to share chemistry with someone, James helped me to remember the positives from my relationship with Brendan – and that taught me a big lesson in love: instead of focusing on all the bad stuff from a past relationship, we should always try to think about what was good. Focus on the positive things about a past relationship and your future ones should be more positive too.

If you struggle to find positives, focus your attention on looking for them next time around. Instead of thinking, 'I hated that about my last relationship', try to think, 'Next time, I'd like someone who can give me …' whatever it is you want. For example your ideal relationship could be with someone who has more spare time than previous partners, or someone who likes walking holidays or who likes to travel. Expand and add to what you would like from a relationship – that's far more exciting than wasting your time focusing on everything that went wrong.

WERE WE, WEREN'T WE?

James and I were pretty much inseparable throughout the season, leaving the press guessing whether we were or were not an item. On the last night at the show's wrap party, he gave me a very special thank you present – the most gorgeous pair of diamond earrings – which to be honest had me wondering if perhaps there had been more than chemistry at play … and then we went our separate ways.

---

2. People come into our lives for a reason

Through James, a long-held belief of my mine was reaffirmed – that the people we meet are sent to teach us things and help us to move forward in life.

I'm sure that James floated into my life to remind me that I would feel chemistry and meet a soul mate again. He also taught me a vital lesson about myself. He was someone who worked extremely hard, and never really took time off. One night, eating sushi with him, I said, 'I can't believe you're not burnt out from working 24/7 the way you do.'

The irony was that I was just the same kind of workaholic as him. Only I couldn't see it at the time! I did go on to burn out – several years later – and it was then that my conversation with James came back to hit me in the face and I realized that, for years, I'd been on autopilot, working round the clock and round the calendar and never giving myself the break I badly needed.

The lessons we learn from the people who come into our lives can always be used to our advantage. We can even learn from seemingly negative experiences. For example, you may wonder why you keep meeting people with emotional baggage, or people who are needy or angry. Well there could be one of two reasons for this:

Either (a) You may have that same kind of baggage and are being shown what that looks like so that you can recognize what needs healing in you by seeing it in someone else.

Or (b) If you don't have that baggage yourself, maybe you are a fixer – someone who likes to rescue others who are weighed down by it.

Now, you may be thinking, 'Why not? What's wrong with trying to fix someone who's broken and needs help?' Well I used to be a fixer, until I realized that the only person I could fix was myself.

We may mean well when we try to help someone to fix their problem – be it anger, depression, alcohol or drugs – but we have to accept that we should not interfere with someone else's journey and the lessons they have to learn. That's not to say that we can't be supportive friends and partners, but the person you want to change has to be the one in charge of the changes. Someone who is hooked on drugs or alcohol can have all the support in the world when they say that they want to give up. I believe the only person in control is the addict, and unless he or she genuinely wants to give up they won't.

Now, when the fixer in me pops back up and I feel the need to help someone, I immediately think of the saying, 'You can lead a horse to water, but you can't make it drink.' So I offer my support, but don't waste my energy trying to fix someone who is not ready to change themselves. I now know that the only thing to come out of that will be aggravation between us – and disappointment when I realize I've wasted all my energy and nothing has changed.

3. With the right mindset, anything is possible

James was the first to admit he was not a natural dancer, but he promised to work as hard as he could – and, as I said earlier, against all the odds we made it to the semi-final!

I was so proud of him as I'd been the one to teach him. But he also taught me a great deal, too. As well as restoring my faith in my ability to recover from my heartache, he taught me to not have tunnel vision. By now I'd spent 30 years dancing, and it had been about the only thing in my life. But James made me see that there was a world of other opportunities out there, and I could grab them without sacrificing my dancing. He already had. He was a businessman, a chef, a TV host and a celebrity. I remember once I asked him how he managed to pack all that in and be in *Strictly*, too. 'It's simple,' he said. 'I just imagine I'm wearing different caps.' He told me that when he was wearing his dancing cap with me, he wouldn't even think about other work. He wouldn't even answer his cellphone, because he knew it would distract him from the matter in hand. He never got sidetracked. I use his example all the time in my own life. Right now, writing this, and when I write my magazine column, I put my writing cap on. Later, when I am coaching, I will wear my life coach's cap.

I now find it helpful to schedule things into my diary and once they're written down, they're written in stone. If I have set aside an hour for a project, then I simply do not allow myself to take any calls, check emails, Twitter or any social media, until that hour is up. Every time you stop to take a call or look at your inbox, you get distracted and it takes time to get back into what you were doing. You will quickly come to realize how much more you can get done when giving each task your full and undivided attention. (When I was writing that, I accidentally keyed in 'divine' instead of 'undivided'! Maybe the universe was trying to tell me something!)

We will often pick out qualities and traits that we recognize from ourselves and it's worth doing this exercise to see if this is the case.

MEETING YOUR EQUAL

When we meet our equals, they are our emotional equals. They do not make us feel that we want to fix them, and they should not want to fix us. James did not need fixing, and though I still needed to heal after Brendan, he knew better than to try and fix me.

A good way to find out whether the person you are considering having a serious relationship with is your emotional equal is to ask yourself these questions:

(a) What are the top qualities about this person?

(b) What are their least attractive traits?

I know it's easier to associate with the positive things we have put down, but when we list the negatives it can be difficult to accept that maybe we, too, have an issue with anger, sadness or negativity, for example. Unfortunately, the fact that we see these traits in others usually means that we possess the same characteristics. Or if we don't now, we probably did in the past.

So, if your partner is constantly moody, take a look at yourself and ask yourself if you are moody, too. It is essential that you be completely honest with yourself here and if you do realize that you are in fact moody a lot, it's time to do something about it. Find out what it is within you that is causing this feeling. Remember, change can only start with ourselves. I have heard people say that after working on improving their own emotions, the people they were irritated by no longer annoyed them.

If you do this exercise and find that you're noticing certain emotions in the other person that you think you once possessed but no longer do, then it could be a reminder of your past that has come back to challenge you – and it may be a sign for you to move on from that person. You are the only one who knows what you need in your life to make you happy and when you dig deep, you will find the answers.

Something I learned from NLP is, 'Perception is Projection', which means that everything you perceive you project. From personal experience I know that this can be a little challenging at first.

Here's a little example of how we can have different perceptions of the same people or situations. You and a colleague or friend both meet the same person at two separate events. The next time you meet up, you tell her what a lovely person you have been introduced to, and she says what a difficult person she has met. Now this could be down to a couple of different things. It could be that the other person has had a rough week or day and your friend has caught her in a different mood than the one she was in when you met her. But it could also be that your friend has some issues and is sometimes rather moody herself and this is how she perceives her new acquaintance.

Or, have you ever wondered why two people who have gone to the same party have had two completely different experiences? I find this fascinating as how they describe the party actually explains a lot more about the person than the party.

Acknowledging an unattractive or unhelpful trait in ourselves is the first step toward changing it. It's like admitting that we have an addiction. I have used hypnosis to help many clients quit smoking. But I have also seen many people resist giving up because although they knew it was not a particularly healthy habit, they still enjoyed it for various reasons: the ritual of opening up a packet; the way they think it makes them look sophisticated in a Bette Davis kind of way; some people actually enjoy the taste! Often some of these clients would tell me how hypnosis hadn't worked for them when they tried – and notice the word 'tried' – to give up.

'But did you really want to give up?' is my usual response to that. 'No!' they say more often than not. 'But I felt like I had to because my partner or friend or whoever told me to,' or, 'I felt like I should, but didn't really want to.'

Let me just be clear about this once and for all: we will not make major changes unless it's we ourselves who decide it's time to change a behaviour trait or habit. We are all on different journeys and we've all got different timetables. So when someone else thinks it's time for you to change something, unless your timetables match, you're not going to. When you do arrive at the conclusion that it's time to change and you have decided that it's time

Change can be powerful, challenging and wonderful because it is going to enhance your life and make you happier, then the change can be powerful, challenging and wonderful.

When we make major changes within I believe that we will often be challenged with a situation to test us to see if the change is fully integrated. For example, if you've recently given up smoking, you may have to face a situation where everyone around you is puffing away – although with fewer and fewer people smoking these days that's increasingly uncommon – and someone offers you a cigarette. I think that's fate's way of testing whether or not you really have given up.

A different scenario could be if you have let go of anger. Let's say you're someone who's on a short fuse, easily wound up and often end up reacting angrily in situations at work or at home. You know this behaviour is doing you no good because when you get angry in situations, you lose perspective and act irrationally.

So you decide to improve your behaviour and in future change all your angry responses to calm ones. This may take some time and you may choose to work with an NLP coach, psychologist or another type of therapy.

How will you know if you have succeeded?

You will more than likely suddenly find yourself in a situation to which you would normally respond angrily. I believe these challenges are thrown at you to give you an opportunity to see if your new behaviour response has become ingrained in you. If you react calmly, well done. If you blew your top, and then become angry with yourself for doing so, don't despair and think, 'Oh well, obviously I was meant to go through life as a bad-tempered curmudgeon.' It just means that psychologically you weren't ready to make the change. But if you persevere, the time will be right. The key to moving forward is always to acknowledge our behaviour and learn from it.

CHAPTER 17
CHEMISTRY

Few of us make it through life without having our heart broken – often several times – and it can be hard to believe that it really is 'better to have loved and lost than never to have loved at all'.

After Brendan, someone told me it would take three years for my heart to heal. That sounded unbearably long, but it also sounded far too short a time, because, at first, I couldn't imagine how I'd *ever* put one foot in front of the other again. That's how heavily my loss weighed on me.

But by season four of *Strictly*, I'd got past that stage. I'd functioned, I'd danced, I'd performed, I'd laughed and I'd even loved – but it was only now that I discovered that my heart still wasn't properly healed after all.

Stormy weather

For this season I'd been paired with the actor Ray Fearon, a lovely, super-talented man who was incredibly conscientious about all our dancing and training. He was in the show because he genuinely wanted to learn to dance. Raising his public profile was not top of his agenda, and he had little time for the frivolities that accompanied the show. When the production team wanted him to go and fly with the Red Arrows to get over his dizziness on the dance floor, he thought it was a total waste of valuable practice time!

And although I understood how footage like that would have made good TV, I was also getting extremely irritated by some of the producers' demands – not just the stunts we were asked to do that were shown in the training slot video on each show before we actually danced, but much more by the way they tried to hint that there was chemistry between us. Keen to get as much media attention as they could, they were trying to whip up stories about us, and interpreting anything they could as a flirtation or a sign that there was more to our relationship than the nation saw on their television screens.

That would have been fine, and I would have played along, only I was now living with Fabio, my on–off lover of three years. He was an intensely private man and didn't want to be dragged into the ridiculous world of celebrity gossip. It really hurt him to see me embroiled in it, too. As well as wanting to protect him from any unnecessary pain, there was also another, deeper, reason I was getting so irritated: all the talk of chemistry between me and Ray brought back unhappy memories of the stories about Brendan and his partner in that awful first season.

Emotionally, I felt as if some invisible hand had picked me up and thrown me three years back in time. I thought I'd dealt with all those feelings when it turned out that I'd just suppressed them. Now they came back to the surface because I hadn't really got angry with Brendan and his partner when it all happened, although it would take me many months to understand that was when I should have screamed and shouted. Instead, I started screaming and shouting now, three years later!

All it took was a little trigger. When the producers tried yet again to hint at chemistry between Ray and me during one of our video packages, I got up and stormed off in tears. Then I called the office and yelled, 'THERE'S ABSOLUTELY NOTHING GOING ON! THERE'S NOTHING BETWEEN US. NO CHEMISTRY! NO ROMANCE! AND THERE'S NOTHING EVER LIKELY TO BE!'

If I thought I was finally seeing the light at the end of the Brendan tunnel, I was wrong. Instead I was suddenly very insecure and angry, so stressed that I started reacting to all sorts of things that I'd normally have taken in my stride.

If the music we'd chosen was changed, I wanted to have a tantrum like a toddler who's been told he can't have an ice cream. I wanted to stamp my feet and shout, 'That's not fair!'

Or, if my schedule got altered – par for the course in TV – I'd question it, even though I knew it was one of those things that was out of my control.

None of this was at all like me. I'd always prided myself on my easy-going and professional nature, and I knew people couldn't help but notice the change in me. My new inflexibility and impatience were signs that something was going on and I needed to deal with it.

As I say, everything happens for a reason – even the bad stuff. You just need to look for that reason, and see how it can help you.

WHAT'S YOUR BEHAVIOUR TRYING TO TELL YOU?

If you're often annoyed by situations or find yourself arguing about things that haven't gone your way, stop and ask yourself: Is your behaviour trying to tell you something? Is there something you need to learn here? Being short-tempered, angry and irritable are typical signs of stress – but your stress may not be caused by that surface irritation. There could be something deeper going on. My behaviour during season 4 was – I'd eventually learn – to do with stress caused by unresolved emotions after my break-up with Brendan, but it also taught me a valuable lesson. When I stepped back and took a good look at myself, I could see that this was exactly how I did not want to act, and – funny how things turn out – I now use the story over and over again when I'm coaching people in business who may find that they react to work situations just like I did back then. Looking back, I am still glad I did put my foot down when it came to the rumours between Ray and me: I did so out of respect for him, and for my own self-respect. I had learned to be flexible, but I'd also learned that it's OK, in fact essential, to set boundaries.

Once I'd realized that this was how I didn't want to act, I decided that for the next season I would work really hard at being more flexible. So I adopted what I called 'standby mode' – essentially going with the flow and adapting to whatever was required of me. I still use 'standby mode' today, whenever I take on a big project that could throw the unexpected at me. Try it – just go with the flow – and see how much smoother everything seems as a result.

As my coach, Tor, had said when he trained Kenneth and me, there are some things outside our control that we can't change and it's not even worth worrying about them because our stress will make no difference.

We all have to learn, especially at work, to put up with schedules being changed, people being late, meetings going badly … the list goes on. Things like that will happen even when we don't want them to, but it's far less stressful if you can just rest in standby mode, and go with the flow.

The way we were

After all the trauma of season four, I seriously considered giving up *Strictly* – but thank goodness I didn't as it was season five that finally saw me healed. But before I tell you about that, I want to talk about Brendan because, between seasons four and five, he asked me to dance with him again.

His call came out of the blue, at a time when we were still just on speaking terms, and only at work. We did become friends eventually but not by then – there was still too much hurt in our hearts. When he told me why he'd called, I couldn't believe what he was saying.

He'd been thinking about taking part in the Eurovision Dance Contest, the dance world's answer to the Eurovision Song Contest, which was to be broadcast on the BBC. However, he still couldn't imagine dancing with any other professional partner but me. Would I, he asked, consider joining him for one last time?

You'd have thought I'd have told him, very politely of course, what he could do! But no, I was actually very touched. Although I was now in an established professional partnership with Ian Waite, there had been a time when I had believed Brendan would be the partner with whom I'd end my days as a professional dancer. And here was Brendan saying that he now wanted to announce his retirement from competition dancing days and he couldn't imagine doing it with anyone other than me. It's a tradition to go out with a farewell dance at one of the big events, which is what he was planning to do, but only if I would partner him.

To me it seemed like accepting would give me some kind of closure, too. After all, when our relationship had broken down, our professional partnership had also come to a very abrupt end.

Both Ian and Fabio understood my reasons for accepting, and off I went. It was strange being in Brendan's arms again for a medley to the James Bond theme tune, and then the rumba, our trademark dance. We danced it to the same tune we'd danced it to all around the world – Barbra Streisand's 'The Way We Were'. The irony was not lost on me! We danced well, but it felt different and we both knew deep down that the chemistry we'd once shared on the dance floor had faded away. There were still so many words unspoken between us, and, when we finished and went backstage to our changing rooms, the tension caught up with us and we both burst into tears. We knew this was the end of what had once been quite magical, but tears can be healing, and as I wiped my face dry I felt the kind of contentment you feel when you have read a good book, closed it, and put it back on the shelf.

Gethin – my healing angel

So now I felt in a much better place for the start of season five of *Strictly* when I was paired with the *Blue Peter* presenter Gethin Jones, someone who practically every woman on the show found sexy and attractive, including me. He was like a caterpillar turning into a butterfly as he slowly allowed me into his personal space and dance hold, without collapsing with giggles.

FIVE THINGS I LOVED ABOUT GETHIN

1. He made me laugh – not from a hurt place, but from a good one and that was so refreshing. We also laughed a lot with the other contestants especially Alesha Dixon and Matt Di Angelo. Laughter is so important to me and after getting to know Gethin, I added laughter to the list of things I like in a man.

2. He tried so hard, and that made me feel that I was a good teacher and doing something right. He picked up all the steps and moves easily and his technique was superb, but on the day, as the judges pointed out more or less every week, his performance was not quite there.

3. He inspired me to act – something I'd wanted to do since childhood, but had left behind in favour of dancing. One week we brought in an acting coach to help him give it that last bit of va-va-voom on the dance floor that we both knew was missing. I later worked with the same

coach when I was learning more about acting myself, so that was another seed sowed for the future when I'd act in the theatre and also use drama in role-play exercises with the corporate clients I coached.

4. He taught me to be more flexible. There was one week that was so seriously stressful, that instead of learning his new routine within two days as he usually did, it just didn't seem to gel. So on the third day we scrapped it completely and started a new one. We worked all night and created something fantastic, which he was totally comfortable about. This was a great lesson for me to learn as coach and as a teacher, especially when I'm coaching people in business: if it isn't working, stop, reevaluate, and don't be too scared to change your strategy. If I had pushed on, forced the situation, and made Gethin dance the routine as it was, it would have been – in the words of the lovely but sometimes scary judge Craig Revel Horwood – 'a disaaaaster, daaaarling!'

5. He made me so proud. I know I helped Gethin to let go and find a new part of himself and that made me feel really good. I think the effort I invested in Gethin, and the rewards I got back in doing so, inspired my current career as a life coach. Diolch, Gethin.

In helping Gethin I had less time to think about my own worries

That season and his fabulous personality lifted my spirit and thanks to him, I could finally feel happiness knocking on my door.

But, still standing between my happiness and me were some unresolved issues, and I eventually had to acknowledge and accept that the reason I had become so het up during season four was all to do with my break-up with Brendan. Those old emotions had come up to the surface for a reason. They had to be dealt with, and, as I hadn't been able to do that myself, I now needed outside help.

Humble pie

Accepting that we need help from someone else can be tough though, especially for people who are successful in their professional lives or are usually very happy and optimistic people. They may not like to admit to what they perceive as a weakness in being unable to deal with problems in one area of their lives.

They think they should be able to handle things on their own. And I was one of these people.

I found it hard because I had always been the type to help other people, always encouraging them to look on the bright

Accepting that we need help from someone else can be tough

side and turn negatives into positives. So you can understand how difficult it was for me to accept that it was now me who needed help. It made me question myself more than a little. But I really did need someone to help me get back on track. And that's when serendipity stepped in.

First, hungry to understand what was going on in my head, I'd started reading book after book about NLP, which is a way of reprogramming our minds and changing the way we behave. I'd used its tools in my sporting life, but never before in my personal one. Then, as luck would have it, my professional partner Ian and I were asked to dance at a charity event where I met someone who practised NLP. Chatting to her, I realized I needed the kind of help someone like her could offer.

So I swallowed my pride, found myself a life coach, and started healing my heart.

It wasn't at all easy though – in fact it was probably one of the most difficult things I've ever had to do. I felt as if I was turning myself inside out, analysing my life, looking under every little stone to see what was there and very often not liking what I found. But I had to do it – if I hadn't I wasn't sure how I would ever properly move on. I didn't want to risk the same old emotions bubbling up unexpectedly again.

Now when I describe coaching and NLP to my clients, I liken it to being on a ship in a very rough sea. You know there will be calm sea ahead, but you don't know how long it will be before you get there.

I felt so vulnerable during this time, and there were moments when I seriously thought about giving up changing anything. It would have been much easier not to let go of my past, my anger, my fear and the deep hurt that I knew was there. I could have stayed just where I was, because horrible as it felt at the time, at least it was something I was used to. The future on the other hand was unknown and slightly scary. When I looked at it, I felt as if I was looking into a void.

Scared to be on my own

One of the most frightening things I had to face up to was the possibility of being alone in the future, but at some point in my therapy I realized that this was just what I needed. I knew that even though I cared for Fabio and had so much respect for him, we had different lives and interests. At weekends, when he was off, I was working. I was spending a lot of time on my own or travelling anyway, and, I had to admit, that I was starting to enjoy that. I came to see that maybe I was only hanging onto the relationship because I didn't want to face being alone, and now it was time to face that fear.

Have you ever done that? Stayed in a relationship that was passed its sell-by date because you're scared of being alone? What I'm going to say may sound strange, but this could be because you, like me, are scared of dying. I know that's a morbid, rather heavy idea to take on board, but as Benjamin Franklin said, death is one of only two things that are certain in life (the other is taxes). When we come to terms with that fear, being alone is no longer anything to worry about.

If you're happy with your own company, that, curiously enough, is something that makes your relationships with others so much better. That's because you choose to be with partners not because you NEED to be with someone, but because you WANT to be with someone in particular.

Therapy helped me understand that my fear of being alone was tied up with an underlying fear of dying: no one wants to *die* alone, no one wants to *be* alone. I also had a fear of flying and of being at sea, these despite having spent countless hours flying around the world and dancing on cruise ships. Therapy helped me to understand that phobias like these are also caused by this fear of death. It can stop us from doing so many things, anything, in fact, that takes us out of our comfort zone, and it can make us stay in a relationship so as not to be alone.

My therapist once told me that we all have to accept that we're born alone and we die alone. If we can learn to love ourselves and start enjoying our own company, then we no longer need to fear dying. Coming to terms with the fear of death is liberating in all sorts of ways. In my case I realized that to move on, I needed to be alone, and to be alone, I needed to break up with Fabio.

I did it as kindly as I could, with complete honesty and utter respect for him. Being the one who has to end a relationship can be as hard and as painful as being the one who is let go. Being kind to your partner when you do it is a way of being kind to yourself, too.

FIVE WAYS TO LEAVE YOUR LOVER

I. Be honest with yourself and your partner: it's quite all right to admit that your lives and expectations are too different for you to be happy with each other.

---

2. Respect yourself and respect your partner and his or her boundaries now, as much as you did when things were going well.

3. Completely resolve one relationship before getting involved in another one. This avoids causing major hurt.

4. Be clear about your reasons for breaking up. Confusion leads to pain.

5. Communicate! Don't expect your partner to guess how you feel.

I learned these valuable points when Fabio and I broke up. We had mutual respect and we each thought the other was a wonderful person. But we also knew deep down that we wanted different things from our relationship. We managed to sit down and have an open conversation about how we felt, about the way our schedules and views clashed. And because we did that, we stayed friends.

When you're in an unhappy situation it's easy to be an ostrich and stick your head in the sand, expecting everything to work itself out. But actually if you find the courage to look your partner in the eye and explain how you feel, the chances are that even if the other person doesn't feel the same or is hurt, they will at least be thankful that you have enough respect for them to have explained exactly how you feel and why you feel that way. If it's done with kindness, respect and sympathy, you will find it much easier to move on without guilt. And if you are the one at the receiving end, then you, too, can move on without feeling anger.

I'm not saying that it's always possible to stay friends, especially in the immediate aftermath of a break-up. But there is definitely a better chance that at least you will not end up resenting each other.

And I always think it helps to heal the pain when we tell ourselves that maybe the universe in fact has something better in store for us.

CHAPTER 18
YIN AND YANG

When you go to buy your groceries, you take a shopping list with you to make sure you buy what you need. But have you ever thought of sitting down and committing to paper exactly what you're looking for in your ideal partner? Actually 'shopping' for what you really want from a relationship, instead of just leaving it up to chance?

After breaking up with Fabio, I decided not to drift into future relationships, but to be proactive about what I wanted in a man.

One of my friends said she'd actually designed her own partner, much as you might design a new kitchen. You may think it sounds a hilarious thing to do – after all, the heart has a mind of its own, and we all say that you can't control who you fall in love with, don't we?

But my friend was so positive about her experience that I decided to try it. I now felt fully healed after Brendan. The Eurovision Dance Contest, doing *Strictly* with Gethin, and my work with the life coach had all helped with that. I'd also spent some time being single, learning to be happy with my own company for virtually the first time in my life, and I felt that I could go into a relationship as an independent woman.

I sat down and wrote my list of top attributes in a man – honesty, kindness, supportiveness, being loving, and then I put it in a drawer and got on with my life.

Somehow this worked like a prayer. It was as if I had placed my order with the universe, and now, without me consciously looking around, the universe provided me with what I had asked for.

DESIGN YOUR IDEAL PARTNER

Don't just dream, act! Write your list down and take it seriously. You may have written some of the following:

- Physically attractive
- Independent
- Loving
- Love of travel
- Loves being with the family and me
- Mutual respect
- Likes to talk and to listen, too
- Financially independent
- Fun
- Makes me laugh
- Honest
- Calm
- Kind
- Easy to talk to
- Wants to spend time together
- Lives in the same city
- Confident
- Mentally and physically available (i.e. not married or in a relationship with someone else!) I had a friend who met her perfect partner ... and then found that he wasn't actually available. When she looked back at her wish list she'd forgotten to specify availability.
  Make sure that you, too, are available, not just physically, but emotionally. Even if you are single, this project will be jeopardized if you have not fully recovered from a previous relationship.

MOST IMPORTANT OF ALL: your list must be what you want, and not what someone else wants for you, or what you think you should want but don't really.

It may also help to make a list of qualities that you can bring to the relationship. I thought I should be able to offer the same things that I was looking for in someone else: honesty, kindness, compassion and respect. I wanted someone who was my emotional equal.

Dog days

Here's what happened. Here's how I finally found the love I craved and the man I deserved. It's another story about fate, and it all starts with my love of dogs!

In 2007, after I'd done *Strictly* with Gethin, I was on a cruise with Fabio and Ian. Ian and I were dancing, Fabio came along to spend some well-earned time off and to be with me for a few, more or less uninterrupted days. When we were at sea, a TV production company sent me an email: would I be interested in taking part in a new reality show? The idea was that a group of celebs would be paired with a dog each, put them through agility exercises and even – guess what – do some doggy dancing with them! The aim was to raise awareness of the Dogs Trust charity, which would supply the doggy dancers and hopefully encourage people to come forward and adopt dogs who needed a new home.

My first thought was that this had to be the best job in the world! I'd never forgotten my lovely dog, Besy. She'd left a gaping doggy-shaped space in my heart, and for years I'd yearned for a furry little character to fill that gap. But I knew I couldn't have a dog with my frantic schedule. I worked and travelled non-stop, and it just wouldn't have been fair. Maybe one day, though.

So when this email came through – asking if I'd train a dog for the summer, I was so, so excited! I couldn't think of anything more amazing than spending all that time with a dog, outside in the fresh air, training and performing.

Unfortunately, I got my hopes up too soon. A few days later a second email came through. The producers had chosen someone else. I was gutted! But, you know what I say about everything happening for a purpose? Well, little did I know it, but once again the universe had a bigger plan in store for me. Have you ever experienced that? Or maybe after reading this you may realize, some time in the future, that something that didn't happen when you wanted it to had given way for something much better to come later on.

This is how I think now, and I've come to realize it's much more helpful than dwelling on what went wrong. As my wise Mor had told me years ago, 'What's for you won't pass you by.' So once again I put my faith in the universe and carried on without giving the dog programme another thought. And then, a year later, the producers contacted me again. I was absolutely thrilled! I was to be one of ten celebs, including the actors Brian Blessed and Lesley Joseph – what an honour! And then another call came through. 'By the way,' someone from the production team said, 'your ex, Brendan Cole, will be on the panel of judges.'

'Uh-oh!' I thought. 'That could be interesting!' We're both fiery people and when fiery people come up against one another … fireworks! But I agreed. 'No problem,' I said. 'I'm fine with that!' After all, we'd worked together for the last five seasons of *Strictly*, so I knew we could be professional about this. And anyway, I was so excited about the job, I really didn't want Brendan to be the spanner in the works that held me back.

On our first filming day we all turned up at the Dogs Trust's centre to be paired with a professional dog trainer – this time I was the one learning instead of teaching, and I loved being on the other side for a change.

My trainer was called Darren and I met him on that first day. I was also asked to pick a dog I felt I had a connection with. There were about five to choose between and I plumped for a gorgeous blond dog called Chico – half Collie, half German Shepherd – probably because the German Shepherd in him reminded me of my Besy.

Being with a dog every day for three months was wonderful. If you're a dog lover you won't need me to tell you how affectionate they are and how special their love can be.

I adored Chico and would have loved to have adopted him at the end of the show – just saying goodbye to him every night when he returned to the dog home was tough – but he was far too big for my apartment, and it would have been unfair to leave him there when I had to work.

But even if I didn't get to take Chico home, he made sure I wouldn't be alone for much longer! As we were leaving our first training session, Chico nuzzled up to one of the other dogs in the show, a dog that looked like an enormous wire-haired Jack Russell. The dog, Sven, turned out to be a Jack Russell crossed with a mix of Staffordshire and English Bull Terrier and had been picked by the actor Kevin Sacre.

As I looked at them both I thought, 'Cute!' (Sven)! 'Handsome!' (Kevin) 'Cocky!' (Both of them!).

What was to happen taught me a lesson. I judged Kevin on his handsome looks and cocky nature and immediately decided that, together with the fact that he was an actor, he must be a bit of a player, and an arrogant one at that. You know what – I was SO wrong – and it was a reminder that you should never judge a book by its cover. When I look back, I feel ashamed at myself for having done that: it was seriously shallow of me. Since then, I've made a determined effort never to gossip, and never to judge. Instead I now try to treat others as I would like them to treat me. It would be a much kinder world if we could all do that – because, the more I read, the more I'm aware that actually we are all one. There's a lovely Scottish expression: 'We're a' Jock Tamson's bairns.' It means that no matter who we are, we're all the same. When we judge others, we are judging ourselves too. And when we see faults in others, we are often seeing the issues that we need to resolve in ourselves.

Anyway, after turning up for training every day for four weeks, as Sven and Chico sniffed around each other in the way dogs do, Kevin and I would always have a casual chat. And I started to realize he was not quite as bad as I'd first thought. He was great with Sven, and as one of my friends remarked when she saw him, 'You learn a lot about someone when you see how they act with an animal.'

The dogs were the stars of the show. Every time the audience applauded, Chico freaked out and tried to run away, something that gave rise to the sort of banter between Brendan and I that the producers were hoping to get. I remember the day I was standing there, frantically waving a treat at Chico to bring him back when Brendan said, 'Camilla, your boy seems out of control!'

'You'd think I'd be used to that by now,' I retorted.

But – back to Kevin. He had an amazing way with Sven. When he got him to jump up into his arms, the audience's 'Oohs!' and 'Aaahs!' told the rest of us that we didn't have a chance. But apart from that, I was starting to enjoy our little chats. He talked about films and festivals and lots of other fun things for which I'd never had time.

At this point, though, I thought nothing more of it. Despite doing my 'Design a Partner' exercise, I wasn't really thinking about having a relationship at that point, or at least I didn't think I was. I was now so focused on the dog show, and although I'd been thinking about a future partner when I was writing down what I wanted in him, I'd thought that it would be nice if I met someone after the next – the sixth – season of *Strictly*, not before it. Though I hadn't actually included that in the list.

So Kevin and I would just chat as friends do. But our lovely fellow contestant Lesley Joseph saw something else in our little *tête-à-têtes*. She'd known us both separately from other jobs – I'd met her on *Strictly*, and Kevin had been in the soap *Night and Day* with her – and she kept hinting that Kevin should invite me out. 'You look so lovely together!' she insisted.

Then, when she saw us walking into the studio together one day, she called out, 'Here comes the lovely couple!'

As I turned to look at Kevin to share the joke, someone asked for our photo. Kevin reached out to put a friendly arm around me, and, as he did that, I got that bolt of lightning that people talk about and suddenly realized that there was something about that guy!

A day or two later he called and asked me out for a drink. 'Oh! That would be nice,' I thought, then said, 'I'd love to.' I did wonder how he'd got my number – it turned out he'd badgered Caren, one of our production coordinators, for it.

It was a lovely date. We went to a place by the river near me and talked and laughed as if we'd known each other for ages. When we stood up to say goodbye we shared a kiss and I could tell that we both felt there was a deep connection. A couple of hours after I got home, Kevin called and said, 'I know this may sound ridiculous – but I'm hoping you feel the same – as far as I'm concerned I'm considering myself off the market.'

'It doesn't sound ridiculous,' I replied. 'I feel exactly the same.'

In the stars?

Now here's the weird thing! Six months before meeting Kevin, we'd both been invited to the same party after a big TV charity event he and I had been involved with. Brendan, who was also involved in the gig, asked me to go with him as a mutual friend had passed away and I think maybe he wanted to be with someone who understood if he was a bit down. But come the end of the day's filming, we'd been working really hard and I was feeling extremely tired. I wanted to be fresh for the following long day's dancing, so I didn't join Brendan for a drink after all. So he went on his own and guess who he spent the night chatting to ... Kevin! He had another girlfriend then and I wasn't at the point where I was ready to meet that special someone. But I couldn't help wondering what would have happened if I had gone to that party and Brendan had introduced me to Kevin. And when I did, I think I knew that my old friend the universe had decided to delay things a little.

Six months later, so much had changed for both of us. Kevin was available, and I was ready for love. After that lovely date by the river, we started going out together. I was still a bit cautious, worried that Kevin wouldn't be able to cope with my hectic schedules, so I wanted to keep it all quiet for a bit. But Lesley soon guessed what was really going on!

Being an actor with a busy schedule – he spent eight years working in soaps like *Night and Day* and *Hollyoaks* – Kevin understood what Fabio never quite could. 'Please don't worry,' he said. 'Just focus on what you have to do and know that I'll be behind you all the way.'

From that moment I knew he was for keeps as well as being a real teammate. Sometimes it's Kevin who's busy and needs my support; other times it's me who needs Kevin's patience and understanding. I feel like we take it in turns climbing a ladder while the other one holds it steady at the base. In a relationship like this there's room for both of us to grow and achieve. And that's pretty much how we make it work.

Strictly over

So my love life was finally on course, but now my professional life needed a bit of TLC. After five years of choreographing, coaching, and performing on TV for half the year, and touring the other half, I was starting to feel as if all my creativity had been sapped. So although my heart was happy, my soul started to suffer. I felt that something had to change, and it was a feeling that took me by surprise when it came. I thought I loved what I was doing, and now I had to admit that maybe I was falling out of love with the only career I'd ever been able to imagine myself doing.

Gut feelings like this are a warning sign, but not everyone pays heed to gut feelings, or is sufficiently in tune with their emotions to recognize them. As a life coach, I now see many business people who've failed to see the warning signs until, wham, bam, they're fully burned out.

Not long before reaching this point, I'd interviewed a couple of retired athletes on a radio show and I'd asked how it feels when you suddenly stop doing the one thing you have lived your life to do? How do you carry on when life as you know it is turned on its head? They said it was like being lost in a forest with no compass. You have to follow all sorts of paths until you find the right one, but you do eventually find it. I knew that even if I was about to enter the forest, I would find the path through it. And I had to believe that the grass really would be greener when I got to the other side.

By this point I had spent 30 years perfecting my dancing, but almost overnight the desire to carry on was gone. I was part of one of the biggest and most successful shows on TV, but suddenly I had no drive or passion to even choreograph one more routine. The most important thing at that moment was to find my inner calm. I'd been on such a journey, learnt so much about myself over the previous five years, that it didn't feel right going back and being faced with my past every time I went to work. I wanted to find out where my passion now lay; what I needed to do to become driven again.

I had to step off the treadmill, take stock of my values and beliefs, and find a new challenge to inspire me. I could probably have stayed in my job, thought about the money, kept my head down and carried on for another five years. But, you see, when you are a passionate person with a competitive background, you have to give what you do 100 per cent or not do it at all.

Being totally honest with myself, I knew it was time to move on, time to find a way to live and work where I felt happy in my soul. I realized that this could mean making some sacrifices and change my lifestyle. But by now I'd been earning a good salary, more than enough to buy the Mulberry bags I'd once sold and the Beauchamp Place dresses I'd once gazed at through store windows, so I was ready to take that risk. Sometimes we have to choose happiness over financial success – and, to me, finding happiness is what success should really be all about. Giving up my, by now, highly successful *Strictly* career had to be worth it if the result was happiness.

So, as I went into season six of *Strictly*, I knew that to stay true to myself this would have to be my last one. And with that in mind, I was determined to give it my best.

I knew nothing about my celeb partner and had just been told to turn up at his home in Clapham where the film crew would be waiting to catch our first meeting. But, standing outside his kitchen door, I spotted a pile of scripts and realized he was going to be an actor. And, when I walked in, it was Tom Chambers from *Holby City*.

When I got home that night I said to Kevin, 'I think I've met the guy I could win with!'

CHAPTER 19

FAREWELL TO ALL THAT

One of the first things I learned about Tom was that he shared my passion for Fred Astaire and Ginger Rogers. And when he confided that he'd always dreamed of dancing like Fred, a light bulb went on in my head and I made it my mission to take this lovely man to the season final for a Fred-and-Ginger style routine.

I felt like I'd been given something precious to hold and told not to drop it. Tom had everything he needed to succeed, and I wanted to make this the best season I'd ever performed in. I was determined to treasure every moment, before I took my final bow and left the series.

Kevin's a great believer in 'living in the now' – focusing on the present moment – and, now I had him in my life, I decided that living in the now would optimize my chances of success.

LIVING IN THE NOW

'Living in the now' is exactly what it says it is. We acknowledge the thoughts about the past and future that come to mind, but we do not dwell on them. When you live in the now, you hear the birds, smell the flowers, taste the wine, feel the breeze ruffling your hair or, put less practically, you immerse yourself in whatever task you have currently taken on. Not only is it hugely beneficial for wellbeing, it also makes you more productive at work.

Kindred spirits

I took each day of season six one at a time, focusing on surviving the elimination at the end of each week. When the camera was on us in close-up, when some couples are told they're going through or that they have to dance off, the tense expressions on everyone's faces, celebs and professionals alike, aren't faked. We all want to go through. That's why I used all the tools I'd learnt through my NLP healing – such as anchoring, hypnosis and visualization – and throughout my years of competing to make sure I was mentally prepared.

Tom was quick to learn and training with him was an absolute pleasure. It was funny, after so many seasons, with so many partners, to find one with whom everything felt 100 per cent right.

We'd spend our coffee breaks talking about our dreams for the future and how we believed in the law of attraction. We had so much in common and that was a tremendous help to our dancing.

I found myself really opening up to Tom. I told him how I'd started studying NLP and wanted to become a life coach, motivating people to follow their dreams and find happiness; I told him how I'd always secretly wanted to act. In turn, Tom told me how he'd always wanted a role in which he'd have to dance as well as act. Just having those conversations made me feel like we were planting seeds. I knew Tom had what it took to dance. He was sure I had it in me to act. Who knew that a few years later I'd land a part in *Calendar Girls*, and Tom would be given the lead in a West End production of *Top Hat*, actually dancing like Fred Astaire. I was overwhelmed with joy when I went to watch him, and the fact that I knew that I had played a part in the huge success he had confirmed my belief in synchronicity – we'd met because we each had something to offer the other.

Kevin and Clare, Tom's wife, became our back-up team, supporting us all the way; and as the weeks ticked by, we realized we were hurtling toward the final.

If they could see me now

It was 12 weeks after the first time we danced on screen and we'd made it to the final three couples – with Brendan and his partner Lisa Snowdon, and Vincent Simone who was with Rachel Stevens.

All the finalists had to rehearse all day every Saturday to ensure that 'lighting and camera' would be perfect when we went out live in the evening, which meant someone had to rehearse winning, too. Now dancers are a superstitious lot and when the cameraman said he needed a couple to pretend to win and potentially hold the trophy none

If we could have seen ourselves then as we were now

of us wanted to tempt fate. But someone had to do it, so we put our names in a hat. It was Tom and I. When the floor manager told us that the winning couple would be dancing to 'Time of My Life' from *Dirty Dancing*, I raised my eyes in disbelief as if to say to God, 'Are you having me on?' for that was the very tune Brendan and his celebrity newsreader had danced to when they won the first season, a time when my life was falling apart. Now, it felt like closure, and if drawing our names from the hat had been tempting fate, this felt like a really good omen. Brendan and Lisa went out first that night. And then it was just Tom and I against Vincent and Rachel. The tune we'd chosen for our last dance was 'If They Could See Me Now' from *Sweet Charity*.

The song meant a lot to both of us. We'd been yearning to get this far. Tom and I had often talked about our early days when we'd had little but hope to keep us going: when he was driving vans and delivering parcels and I was dusting shelves in Mulberry. If we could have seen ourselves then as we were now ...

When Tess Daly sent us on to the stage with the words, 'This is your chance!' I knew everything was riding on the next few minutes. But we really lost ourselves in the dance, really lived in the now, and it felt so wonderful that, when we finished, I thought that even if we left with the trophy, the evening couldn't get any better than it already was.

But, a few minutes later, when Bruce Forsyth, a man I love to bits, announced, 'And the winner is ...' his words followed by the usual dramatic pause, my heart felt like it had paused, too, in one of those protracted moments when you can't believe you'll ever get to hear what comes next.

Then it happened. 'Tom and Camilla!' I flung myself at Tom, both of us hugging, crying, laughing and jumping up and down on the spot, and moments later, there we were, tears still wet on our cheeks, dancing to 'Time of My Life', and it was the perfect end to my *Strictly* career. Brendan was there to witness it and sitting in the front row, by complete coincidence, was his celeb partner from season one.

Saying goodbye

A few days later I broke the news that I would not be returning to the show. My decision attracted plenty of criticism. 'How can you leave the best show on TV?' people asked. 'How can you go when you're right at the top?' I wasn't surprised. I didn't expect them to understand that unfortunately, after five years, I couldn't grow any further with the brand, and needed to move on from a job that was a constant reminder of the most painful episode of my life.

Truth be told, deep down I wished there was some way I could have stayed with *Strictly* – as a judge, maybe, or as a presenter.

But there weren't any openings at the time, and leaving the show was the only way I could now change direction.

Fortunately, as well as critics I had my supporters who told me how brave I was. Brave because I was giving up the security of lucrative regular work and stepping into the unknown. And that, as I know as a life coach, is one of the hardest things any of us can do.

Leaving *any* job when you don't have another one lined up is always tough – even if that job is low paid and bad for your morale. But leaving a job that you enjoy, one that has shaped your career, brought you fame, made you a household name? Who does that when they don't have something much better to go to?

But I had to listen to my soul and it was telling me that I was no longer happy and no amount of fame or money could change that.

I needed a break, and I needed it so badly that the minute I announced my departure, I felt as if a tidal wave of tiredness had caught up with me, a wave that had been building up for months without me noticing. But now, with that announcement, I'd let down the barrier that had been holding it at bay.

I had been working pretty much seven days a week for the previous five months. But before I gave in completely and could find the time to flop on my bed if that's what I wanted to do, Tom and I had to complete a two-month *Strictly* tour – dancing in London, Manchester, Nottingham, Birmingham and Glasgow.

It felt like a really long, drawn-out goodbye – the kind when you just want to get in the car and drive off, but keep on remembering that you've left something behind and keep having to go back. And it wasn't made any easier that everywhere we went people kept telling me, 'You're mad to leave! Why are you doing it?'

Thank goodness my skin had got thicker over the years. 'B***** to them,' I thought. 'What gives them the right to think they know what feels right for me? How do they know what my dreams and desires are?' Just because I had danced for most of my life didn't mean that I had to carry on doing it for the rest of it.

Giving love a chance

As well as feeling more tired than I had thought possible, there was also another reason for leaving, and one that I shared with nobody else. I thought it was a good time to leave because I had found a man who I felt deeply deserved someone who could take a day off once in a while. I knew I needed to develop a good work-life balance. I decided to live in the now as I gave myself time to work out where my life was going to take me next.

For the length of that final *Strictly* tour, I felt as if I was fighting a cold. I was worn out and run down. I was emotionally wrung out, too. Back in the dressing rooms on the night of our very last performance, Lilia Kopylova gave me a lovely farewell card and gift, but as we went to take up our positions on stage and she reached out to hug me, I had to put my hands up to stop her. 'Don't,' I said. 'I'm only just holding it together. If you hug me I'll cry.'

I'd known Lilia since I was 16. She ignored what I'd said, and, as the music started, she gave me a huge hug. Peeping out over her shoulder I caught sight of Ian, who was also on the tour, and the tears started to roll down my cheeks. But they were tears of contentment as well as sadness. It was a beautiful moment of closure, and, when Tom and I finished our last dance together, I knew I was ready to go.

CHAPTER 20
BURN OUT

A few days later I was on a plane, flying to Dubai with Kevin for a much-needed holiday. I was really looking forward to it, but you know how you can keep going until you give your body permission to rest? That's what I was doing. I was like a car running downhill on an empty petrol tank. When it gets to the bottom of the hill, it comes to a stop.

One night when we were having dinner in a lovely restaurant, I looked at Kevin and said as I toyed with my food, 'Baby, I'm so exhausted I could cry.'

'That's OK, Baby,' he said, his face soft with kindness and understanding. 'Don't give yourself a hard time about it.' He'd been working non-stop for eight years, so he knew exactly what it was like to feel so shattered.

We analysed what had been happening. When I started *Strictly* in 2003, I'd come straight from years of competing, and I'd never had a proper rest since.

This holiday recharged my batteries a bit, but it wasn't until months later that I realized how much more time I really needed to give myself.

Whatever next?

Back home in Surrey, I decided to find the time I'd promised myself to complete the NLP and hypnosis courses I'd started before the *Strictly* tour in 2009, the one with Tom. I saw it as a sabbatical from my normal working life, but, as often happens when I decide to take a break, new opportunities flooded in, including being asked to do my fitness DVD, *Dance Off The Inches*. But something had changed. Somehow I couldn't muster my usual drive or motivation. I felt creatively empty, as if I'd lost my mojo, and I didn't like it. I only knew how to work. Even since I was a child, I'd never had much time for relaxation. And now I asked myself, if I couldn't get as excited as usual about work, then what was left?

I was in a state of flux. Did I want to leave show business and move into full-time motivational work? And if it was the latter, how could I motivate others when I couldn't even motivate myself? I remember that at the time I had this deep feeling of loss inside: more than loss, emptiness. I was shocked that the enormous drive I had always had, that had taken me from a two-year-old with a clumsy foot to a professional dancer at the very top of her profession, had gone. And I was terrified in case it never came back.

Flux was soon replaced by limbo! I couldn't see the reason for anything. I was burned out. I realized that after years on the treadmill, going round and round more and more frantically like a hamster on its wheel, it would take a lot more than a week in Dubai to put the wind back in my sails.

Thank God for Kevin. He totally understood that. He knew I just needed time. Having said that, maybe *he* was another reason I felt less inspired in my professional career. Our life together was so wonderful that it really put into the shade any joy I could ever hope to get from my work. In fact, being with Kevin, for the first time in any relationship, I could see that marriage would add something to my life and that it would trump simply living together. True, I'd always said to Brendan that I didn't need a ring on my finger to prove my commitment. But then Kevin told me, not once but often, what a wonderful thing he thought marriage was. 'Look at our parents,' he'd say. 'They've been together over 40 years. Isn't it beautiful to have that kind of commitment and grow old together.' And when he said that, I found myself wanting that commitment and secretly wishing he'd ask me to marry him. I'd come to realize that to commit yourself to another person for the rest of your life has to be the ultimate way to express your love.

I had no idea what plans Kevin had in mind, but after we'd been at Erin Boag's wedding in Positano, on Italy's Amalfi coast, we went on to Capri for a few days on holiday. It's such a beautiful island and I loved it so much that I wanted to show it to Kevin. It was there that I found myself thinking wistfully how romantic it would be to get engaged there. It came as a huge surprise when the thought came into my head – but there it was!

Then as if reading my mind, Kevin kept joking about what a beautiful, romantic place Capri was. 'I wish I'd thought of it sooner,' he said. 'If I had, I could have proposed to you here. Shame I don't have a ring. Would a Haribo do instead?'

To commit yourself to another person for the rest of your life has to be the ultimate way to express your love

I thought we were both having a laugh. If I'd had even an inkling that getting engaged was on Kevin's mind, the way he was joking about it would have banished the thought from my head. Little did I know!

After we'd been there for a day or two, we were walking down a cliff path to an idyllic beach when he suddenly went down on his knees. Thinking he was still fooling around, I begged him to get up. 'It's not funny, Babe!' I said. And it wasn't. But how was he to know that his pulling my leg was ruining my fantasy proposal.

But this time he wasn't pulling my leg, he was pulling something out of his pocket. And, when I saw what it was, I gasped. He was holding the most beautiful ring I'd ever seen – a Tiffany princess-cut diamond, with smaller diamonds around the centre one. It was stunning, delicate and elegant, exactly the ring I would have chosen for myself!

Then he stopped smiling. 'Will you marry me?' he asked with a serious look on his face.

As I answered with a resounding 'Yes!' my sunglasses were sent flying through the air as I threw my arms around him. I don't think I've ever wanted anything more in my life.

And this time, unlike the last time I'd got engaged, we started planning our perfect wedding day right away. The following summer, we decided. In Ibiza.

I'm A Celebrity

Strictly had catapulted me into the world of celebrity, where the phone would ring and someone would ask, 'Are you up for a project we're planning?' That was how I'd got *Underdog*, the TV show where Kevin and I had met, as well as the fitness video, the Aristoc endorsement, the CBBC show *Dance Factory* and many other projects; and it was how, just after I got engaged to Kevin, I was invited onto *I'm A Celebrity ... Get Me Out Of Here!* I jumped at the chance. What was I thinking?

Spiders, snakes, dark tunnels, foul smells, jungle grub challenges; I had no idea what I was letting myself in for. And yet I thought I had prepared myself perfectly! I was given a month's warning only, but during that time I'd used hypnosis to help feel comfortable with rats and creepy-crawlies. But when the producer said to me, 'There won't be much food out there,' I can't have been listening properly!

Diet-wise, the most preparation I'd done was to wean myself off coffee, because I didn't want to be the grumpy one craving her caffeine fix. And I thought I could avoid any headaches, too. But food? Somehow I completely forgot how much it means to me! I've got a fast metabolism and a big appetite, but I'm also used to eating little and often to fit in with dancing. But eating little and often wasn't something that fitted with life in the jungle where there would be nothing to snack on and everything would be rationed to a few paltry portions of tasteless rice and beans.

Along with the other contestants I was taken to Sydney's Gold Coast, but we were all put in different hotels and not allowed to meet for a few days. The producers wanted to ratchet up the tension, and leave us guessing who the others would be. Then, the moment of truth came, and we were all introduced to each other on a boat. And what a great group it was. Among the celebs who I'd be sharing jungle life with were Hollywood star George Hamilton, the TV chef Gino D'Acampo, the singer Samantha Fox and eight or nine others.

We were divided into three different groups. One had to hike into the camp, one skydived and my group rode in on horseback. So far so good.

Two days after we had all arrived at the camp, and shortly after the show had gone live in the UK, Katie Price arrived too. She'd done it before, and the public voted for her to do practically every task in her first week, so the rest of us were just hanging around, feeling a bit flat.

I don't think I'd ever sat around for five days just doing nothing. I was so bored. Looking back, maybe it was a sign from the universe that I needed to learn to sit still and just be. And it wasn't just the boredom, I was starving all the time. It was so unbearable that one day when we were given a water melon to share, a few of us actually considered eating the skin.

It was literally beans and rice three times a day, supplemented by whatever the producers decided to reward us with – which was still not as lot – when someone completed one of the gruesome tasks they'd been asked to do.

With the fire blasting out smoke all night, sleep was hard to come by, and as for going to the loo, still wearing a microphone and with just a piece of canvas between you and the camera, that really was the pits!

Strangest of all though, was how you adjust to these things quite quickly and they start to feel normal. Even so, I knew something wasn't right when I started getting a desperate craving for bananas. I'd had it before when I was a dancer and I was low on sugar. But from the moment I started craving bananas in the jungle, it was downhill all the way. When I started getting bad cramp in my hands, I knew it was a sign of mineral deficiency. When I was desperate for something sweet, Sam [Fox] gave me some jam she'd somehow smuggled in from one of the tasks, but it wasn't enough.

Early in the fourth evening, when I'd been in the diary room and been asked about a conversation I'd had with some of the other contestants, I couldn't remember their names or what we'd talked about. This was a very scary moment for me. Later that night Katie Price said she could tell I wasn't well and offered to top and tail with me in her camp bed. 'I'm used to it with the kids if they are not well,' she said. 'So just wake me up if you need me.'

A few hours into the night I felt my breathing was getting tighter, my hands were cramping badly and I didn't feel at all like myself. I lay there thinking about what had happened in the diary room and I started to feel as if my mind was going. That will rank as one of the scariest moments in my life for some time.

In the middle of the night I woke Katie and said I was feeling really ill. Being the lovely, kind person she is, she walked me up to the diary room and sat with me until the doctor came. She was still totally jetlagged, trying desperately not to drop off. I'll never forget what a gem she was that night.

The doctor gave me something to help me sleep and the next morning when I saw her again we agreed that I couldn't go on with the show: I had to be sent home. I was given food and drink and two days later when I was fully rehydrated, I was on a flight back to England, heading for home.

I hated having to leave early. I know it made me look like a quitter, and that was one thing I'd NEVER been! And I hated letting the others down. But I had to accept defeat. I chose my health over a TV show and I could live with that.

As soon as I was out of the jungle I called Kevin and my Mor. They were both so relieved to hear my voice because apparently they had seen some footage of me crying live on air. 'Thank goodness you are out,' Mor said. 'I've been praying that you wouldn't stay. You looked so unwell, I was seriously worried about you.'

And apparently when I talked to Kevin on the phone, I sounded so dreadful, delirious almost, that he told me later that he'd hardly understood a word I'd been saying, 'You sounded as if you were talking in your sleep,' he said.

For two weeks, I was unwell and almost too weak to move. Kevin slowly helped me to regain my strength with my favourite dishes like his home-cooked salmon, lamb and chicken. When I was stronger, he told me there had been some bad press and that some people had been saying some really unpleasant things about me, like that I obviously had some sort of eating disorder. He'd been really upset and wanted to defend me somehow. He knows I love food and was angry that word was going around that I was constantly on a diet.

Funnily enough, I didn't get as upset as Kevin about it. I just thought, 'I know the truth and that's all that matters.'

Enough is enough!

Although I am the biggest fan of *I'm A Celebrity* and I adore Ant and Dec, I just had to admit that my body wasn't suited to what it was being asked to go through. I think in life it's quite OK to throw your hands in the air and say, 'Well, at least I tried', because if I hadn't given it a go I would have wondered what it would have been like, and it might have ended up being the best thing I'd ever done.

Sometimes fear of the unknown holds us back from trying something new, so I'm proud that I went for it because although I fell ill, I also have some amazing memories from the four days spent in the jungle – the laughter, dancing with everyone around the campfire, the friends I made. And I learnt a valuable lesson about what my own limitations are. I now know that I'm happy to take on challenges as long as I have my food and my sleep!

GIVE YOURSELF A BREAK

After *I'm A Celebrity*, I realized that I hadn't fully recovered from the burnout I'd had before I'd embarked on the show. I didn't know that at the time, but I learned from the experience that I mustn't let myself burn out again. Now, if I feel stressed or need inspiration for a project or speech, I simply take some time out, anything between 5–20 minutes, to meditate.

You may be thinking, 'I could never do that', but believe me, if I can do it anyone can. I used to find it so hard to sit quietly for even five minutes. My mind would race away and I would be thinking of 101 things at one time, making plans about tomorrow, next year, whatever, but eventually I taught myself to just take five minutes. It helps to join a meditation group, or if you prefer to be on your own, you can find a guided meditation on the Internet. Or you can do what I do – just sit with your eyes closed, allowing thoughts to come and go, not paying any attention to them. Sometimes my five minutes became 10 or 20, but I was happy even if it was just the five. Taking this time now gives me the inner calm I need to see me through the rest of the day, and meditation definitely helped me change my life, to be more calm and keep the creativity flowing.

SO, TAKE FIVE MINUTES ...

Sit on the floor, cross your legs, and rest with your hands palms-up on your knees. Close your eyes and focus on your breath going in and out. I find it helps to have some soft music in the background. Ask in your mind what it is you're looking for: inspiration maybe or the guidance to see through a project you're involved in. When the five minutes are up, open your eyes and take a few deep breaths to bring you back, and as you do this, be thankful for the inspiration to carry on with your day, for it's more than likely that things will flow just that little bit easier because you have given yourself the gift of being calm. Remember what Matthew wrote in chapter 7, verse 7 of the Bible: 'Ask, and it will be given to you; seek, and you will find; knock, and the door will be opened for you.'

CHAPTER 21

WHEN ONE DOOR CLOSES

There were two ways of looking at my speedy exit from the jungle: (a) I could feel sad and disappointed that my body had let me down and I couldn't stay the course; or (b) I could remind myself there was nothing to be achieved by sitting around feeling sorry for myself, and – as Mor and Far always used to say, 'If you fall, get up and brush yourself down.' So I knew I had to try and do that and get ready for the next opportunity to come my way. And it did. Just days after leaving the show, my manager called about another project and I realized that leaving *I'm A Celebrity* was all part of a bigger, better plan for me. It was as if the universe was saying, 'Don't worry. You did your best. But you had to come out of *there* to be *here* for this.' And 'this' was a second fitness DVD, one that would tie in perfectly with another project my manager had already lined up – a daily 'Dancing Queen Diet' slot on GMTV – where I'd be live in different locations every day during the January detox season, when everyone tries to get back into shape after the Christmas party season.

I almost burst with excitement when I found out that one of my GMTV locations was the ballroom at Blackpool Tower – the very place where my dream had started when I was 12 years old. I was jumping with joy, thinking about how, if I had never come to the UK, never auditioned for *Strictly*, and never retired from the show when I did, none of this would ever have happened. I'd had my dreams, I'd acted on them, believed in them, and I had succeeded in making them come true.

Taking that leap and leaving *Strictly* had its scary moments – if I'd listened to all the negative reaction to my decision and taken it to heart, my confidence could have been knocked sideways and I don't believe that I would have been open to the opportunities that then came my way.

When I left, I had no idea that all these lovely offers would come through for me. But they had, and I would never have known how my life would change if I hadn't been so courageous.

But I also learned something else about myself when I left the show. With hindsight, I could now see that for the years that I'd been immersed in it I'd become the friend that nobody wants to be: the one who never had time to talk on the phone or go to important birthday parties, even weddings; the friend about whom others would say, 'Don't tell Camilla – she's too busy!'

Now or never

With Kevin in my life, and my new determination to live in the now, I knew this had to change. I would make more time for the people who mattered – and especially the person who mattered the most: Kevin. Between us we decided one of the best ways we could live in the now was that we'd plan and organize our wedding together, instead of handing it over to wedding planners. You may think that with the wedding over a year away, that sounds like living in the future. But when you live in the now, you cherish each individual act that you take on. Whether it was selecting invitations, writing the guest list, or planning the menu, we immersed ourselves in the tasks in hand, and that kept us rooted in the present, while at the same time making us excited about what we knew would be the best day of our lives.

Where possible, we involved friends and relatives, too, and that was a lovely way to stay connected with the other people we cared about. For example, we both wanted a beach wedding and had decided on Ibiza, as that's where we'd spent our first holiday together. But instead of just plumping for a hotel from a brochure, we tasked one of my best friends and one of my bridesmaids, Andrea, with tracking down a beautiful beach restaurant from a picture I'd found on the web! People loved having a special part to play, and it meant a lot to me to have friends like Andrea involved in our plans.

My manager told me that *Hello!* magazine, who'd already taken some photos of our engagement, wanted to cover our big day – what an honour! But we didn't want that to depersonalize our day so we canvassed our friends and family to make sure they were cool with the idea before going ahead.

The magazine arranged for my sister, Jeanet, and her daughter Michaela – who was then 11 and really excited about being my bridesmaid – to join me for a lovely pre-wedding shoot where they had a chance to be dressed up and styled like celebs. Seeing the joy that brought them gave me huge pleasure, too. That was the moment that made me feel that my success was worthwhile – all those years of hard work meant so much more when I could share my rewards with my family.

The shoot took place in one of the boutiques I used to dream of shopping in during my impoverished 'beans on toast years', when I was working in the Mulberry store – and it was also in that, to me, really special boutique that I chose my beautiful Suzanne Neville dress. It was a fantasy gown – simple at the top, just narrow shoulder straps and a fitted bodice, but then it cascaded down to the ground, glowing with pearls. It was the very last style of dress I thought I would choose for myself! You see, although I am known on TV for my sparkles, that's just part of my showbiz persona – as I said earlier, the glam and glitz are all part of the job. Off-stage my style is far, far simpler.

But this was the first dress I saw when I entered the store and though I reached out and stroked it, I wanted something simpler. Or thought I did. But a dozen or so dresses later and none of them seeming to be quite right, I was beginning to despair, when my Mor and Far said, 'What was wrong with the lovely one you seemed to like when we came in?'

So out it came, and as soon as I tried it on, we all knew it was the perfect dress for me! And guess what! I even had Swarovski crystals on my veil, and that this was after having been adamant that there would definitely not be any sequins or crystals on my wedding day. What makes me laugh about this is that I'd touched that dress, been drawn to it as soon as I saw it, and yet I'd tried to fight my instinct to go with it. I don't know why I did that. As you know by now, I am someone who places so much store by my instinct and intuition. If I'd listened to my heart, the task of choosing my dress would have been over in five minutes! Because, when you live in the now, have confidence in yourself, and trust your gut feeling – all the things I have been talking about – everything just falls into place effortlessly. Life is easy, comfortable and full of delights.

Needless to say, having planned our own wedding, and involved our closest friends and family, it was the most magical day we ever could have wished for. I know it sounds cheesy, but it really was like being in a fairytale.

After the wedding, we went off to the Maldives, taking two whole weeks off work – something I had never done before! Kevin said that we should both use the time to recharge our batteries as well as enjoying lazy days together. 'Switch off your phone, and put it in the hotel safe,' he said. Oh, what a wise man I had married. I even took yoga and meditation classes every day, so I really wound down. And that was just what I needed because when we got back, I had a new challenge waiting for me.

Calendar girl

Since being inspired by Tom Chambers, I'd been taking acting classes, and when Kevin and I got back from honeymoon I went straight back to them. While I didn't know how long it would take before I'd be ready to audition for an acting job, I just knew that one day I would be an actor, but only because I was putting in the groundwork and sowing the seeds! I've never believed in leaving things to chance.

Little did I know, however, that there was a job just around the corner and it had my name on it. Here's what happened, how serendipity stepped in yet again ...

Kevin had auditioned for a part in *Calendar Girls*, the stage version of that wonderful film that starred Helen Mirren and a host of other great British actors. The play was touring the UK, and the producer David Pugh said to Kevin, 'How's Camilla doing since leaving *Strictly*?'

'Oh she's doing great,' Kevin said. 'All sorts of different TV gigs and dreaming about doing theatre one day, too.'

He thought no more about the conversation, but, without consciously planning it, he'd planted a seed for me. A couple of weeks later, I got a call to ask if I'd like to audition for the show – playing quirky Elaine. She's the frivolous and carefree beautician who lives for the moment but never thinks about the consequences of what she does. (The fact that she was exactly the opposite to me, made me think that, perhaps, I should take myself a little less seriously sometimes!) If I got the part, I'd also be understudying Celia Imrie, the lady behind the buns! I hadn't even finished the audition before I was offered the job. And when I started, not only was I working alongside Kevin, who was doubling up, playing the photographer and also a marketing guy up from London, but also our lovely friend Lesley Joseph, who'd played Cupid when Kevin and I had met.

I couldn't have wished for a better start to my acting career. For the four months left of the tour, I was made to feel loved and supported in my new adventure.

BE READY WHEN THE OPPORTUNITY COMES ALONG

When I started thinking about making the transition from dance to drama, I took elocution lessons to improve my accent and pronunciation, and discovered to my embarrassment that I called dresses 'frogs' not 'frocks'– rather awkward when you work in a fashion house such as Mulberry! Even more embarrassing, for years I'd been asking people round for 'drinks and nipples'.

I also took singing lessons, and found out that I had the kind of voice that was better suited to show tunes than the kind of pop I would have preferred. During *Strictly* I wanted to know what it felt like to be a complete beginner at something, like my oh-so-brave and gallant partners. So to put myself in their shoes, I agreed to perform a song at a charity gala evening. I decided to sing 'Making Whoopee', which I sung, just like Michelle Pfeiffer had done it in *The Fabulous Baker Boys*, lying across a piano. In the process of getting it together, I learned I'd taken on quite a commitment and that if I really wanted to be good at it, I needed to do two things. First, I needed to spend money on lessons, and, second, I needed to rehearse, otherwise my money would be wasted.

It was something I was willing to do though, even if it meant saving the money for the lessons. When I am talking to clients about changes they want to make, I often hear excuses like, 'I couldn't afford to do that.' But, when you start to think outside the box and learn to be creative, you probably can find a way to afford it. It may mean making sacrifices in other areas of your life, like living in a less pleasant part of town or taking on extra hours at work. If you really do not have the money, and are already stretched to the limit, you could look for someone who will teach you what you want to learn in return for something that you can teach them, maybe a language you're fluent in or a skill you've acquired. If your dream is worth living, it is also worth this investment. Remember: where there's a will, there's a way! If you really, really want something, you'll find a way to get it; if you only *think* you want something, the chances are you won't.

In at the deep end

I learned so much on the job, that touring *Calendar Girls* was more like going to drama school than being thrown in at the deep end. Kevin and I took our dog Sven – the Jack Russell cross Kevin had done *The Underdog Show* with and that we'd adopted when it was finished – on tour with us. We travelled through the glorious British countryside, staying in holiday cottages and dog-friendly hotels; and despite performing in eight shows a week, touring with my loved ones there were plenty of times when it felt like an extended holiday. I woke up exhilarated every day, thinking how grateful I was and how glad that I'd shared my dream with my husband, who had then shared it with the producer.

Are you a sharer? I think it pays to be open, because that's how things come through for us. But I would say, 'share with care'. I have found that there are some people I instinctively know not to share with because their own negative thinking can be toxic and put a damper on my dreams. When you meet someone, you soon get to know if it's a person you can trust enough to ask for help. If I was looking for a plumber, or a decorator or a dressmaker, I'd ask everybody I know if they could recommend someone. But I don't tell everyone what my inner dreams are: I tend to share these with my more optimistic friends, knowing that their optimism will rub off on me. I am a true believer in the sayings, 'Don't ask, and you won't get' or 'Nothing ventured, nothing gained!' But just be mindful whom you ask.

In other words, instead of worrying, 'Will so-and-so think I'm mad if I say that I'd really like to learn a new language, move abroad, get a job in the film industry, whatever,' just come out and say it. Be open and the world will open up to you.

On *Calendar Girls*, I met wonderful like-minded actors who helped open my eyes to the world around me. Sue Bovell shared my belief in the law of attraction, while Jane Lambert was writing a book, just as I'd always yearned to do, so really I like to think that leaving *Strictly* led to me meeting Kevin, which led to me getting *Calendar Girls*, which led to me meeting Jane, and this finally brought about this book that I'd dreamed of writing since childhood, and that Kevin and my manager Maria had both urged me to do.

That one tour of *Calendar Girls* became four – and a total of two years of going round the country four months at a time, with my husband and dog – but I know that despite all the seeds being sown, I'd never have managed to go on stage if it hadn't been for all the hypnosis I did to prepare for it. My voice would have tightened with nerves; I would have got flustered and forgotten my lines. Even so, the first time I stepped out on stage my knees were knocking – I was so nervous.

HYPNOSIS

The first time my therapist mentioned hypnosis to me, I imagined she could have me hopping around and croaking like a frog … but it's actually more like a series of deep relaxation exercises, like being in the same kind of trance you go into when you're driving and can't remember how you got from one place to the next, or when you're watching TV and don't take in what's happening. While you're in this state, the therapist can work with your subconscious mind to help you change a habit or solve a problem that your conscious mind is struggling with.

On my second ever performance, I managed to get my heel caught in a gap in the floorboards. I couldn't move and nearly froze with fear.

I thought, 'Come on, Camilla, think quickly!' and then I remembered how I'd once lost a shoe in a competition and had to kick off the other one and dance barefoot. So, in character as Elaine, I went shoeless, thinking, 'Welcome to the world of acting!'

Having to sing in pantomimes was even more nerve-racking. Even though I'd taken lessons I didn't feel entirely confident, but I just had to get on with it. Already determined to make a career as a life coach, I told myself, 'If I can pull this off, then I'll be in a far better place to help others!' And indeed, I recently worked with a very inspiring businessman who admitted he spends most of his life outside his comfort zone, doing things that don't immediately come easily to him. I thought to myself, 'That's exactly how I feel!' For me, it is the only way to learn and grow. This is how you make your dreams a reality – by acting on them and believing you can do it. As I always say, 'Jump ... and then learn to swim!'

New directions

All those chats with Sue about the law of attraction, and with Jane about writing a book, convinced me that the next task on my to-do list had to be getting proactive about life coaching. In my spare time I'd now qualified as a master NLP practitioner coach, and hypnotherapist; and then – via Twitter and my management company – I let people know that I was now available to give motivational talks, and opportunities started opening up. Behind the scenes I was working on this book and seeing clients (some of whom were household names) for confidential one-to-one sessions, as well as working with businesses that wanted to motivate their staff. Sometimes I'd work with teams, teaching them how to communicate more effectively, find harmony within a team, and how to feel relaxed outside of their comfort zones. I remembered the lessons I'd been taught by my dance coaches and through my business studies, and wished I'd had the benefit of a life coach earlier in my career.

THIS IS WHAT SUCCESS FEELS LIKE

I'd won awards for dancing, including the coveted *Strictly* trophy. But this reference that one of my business clients, Alastair Clifford-Jones, put on LinkedIn for everyone to see, meant just as much to me. We both knew that his staff would have been sceptical when he'd said, 'I'm bringing in a professional dancer from *Strictly Come Dancing* who's now a life coach to do some motivational work with you,' but he had faith in me – believed, as I do, that you should not judge a book by its cover. I treasure the words he wrote for my professional website:

'As a rapidly growing organization based all over the UK with large customer commitments, we don't often get the opportunity to meet and bond as a team. Feedback from company surveys had indicated that communication was something people felt needed attention, and we therefore booked Camilla to provide coaching and team-building for our organization at our head office based in Oxfordshire.

'Camilla provided one-to-one confidential coaching sessions with each team member to understand their thoughts about the company, the management team, their role and their colleagues. From these sessions a full day of team-building was developed in partnership with management, using Camilla's skills as an NLP practitioner.

'Camilla was able to quickly build a fantastic rapport with every member of the team and was able to engage and motivate through a series of activities that took everyone out of their comfort zones. Camilla enabled us to work together and understand the importance of each member's role to be successful.

'Despite initial scepticism, feedback from the entire company has been incredibly positive and everybody involved felt that the individual sessions and the team-building day was a worthwhile experience. The day was filled with fun and laughter and people engaged in all the activities and sessions wholeheartedly.

'Camilla is unique in her approach, sharing personal experience and injecting her own infectious personality and humour into the journey. I would highly recommend Camilla to any company or individual looking to step outside of the norm and take a different view in order to achieve success.'

My career was taking a new and exciting direction, and so was my personal life – literally! Kevin and I started to talk about moving to Los Angeles, when one day a dancing friend of mine, Julian, called. I'd known him since he was 12, when Brendan and I were his dance coaches. When he was older, he became one of my life-coaching clients and moving to LA was his dream, too. In fact, he'd already set himself a timetable, which really impressed me, for I believe that when you have a dream or a plan it helps to make it happen if you say, 'I'll do this in X months' time.' There's no point making a ten-point plan if you don't do anything to see it through. So we said to Julian, 'You go ahead and when you are settled we'll join you.' It was like making a promise, and that helped to galvanize us to make that move. A year later, Julian phoned and said, 'I'm in LA and I've now reached all the goals you've ever helped me set, including being part of *Dancing with the Stars* [the US version of *Strictly*]. Now it's *your* turn. When are you coming out like you said you would?'

What he said cemented our plan, and that night Kevin and I sat down and worked out what steps we had to take to make it a reality. Something as big as that doesn't happen overnight. Maybe you've made a big move in your life, or maybe you dream of doing so – either way you probably know that, to make it work, you need to put various things in place. First we needed money. We worked out it would take us a year to save

If you really, really want something, you'll find a way to get it

up for the move and looked into the sacrifices we'd have to make to get it together. Then we found out about applying for visas and all the other practicalities.

Some people thought that when we turned up in LA, we'd jumped on a plane, spur of the moment. Of course we hadn't.

We'd made a plan and stuck to it. We'd put all our belongings into storage, rented our house out, and lived out of a suitcase while we got the money together. We also had to find a way of taking Sven with us, and where to live when we got there. There was so much to do, but we did it. We're living in a complex of apartments with its own gym and pool, and surrounded by a lot of like-minded, creative and spiritually aware people, which was the very thing that had attracted me to LA in the first place.

Being there fired my ambition to finish this book, and doing so in the sun became my real vision. Making that vision a reality, achieving that major goal was something I felt I had to achieve if I was to speak with complete conviction to my clients when talking about them achieving their goals.

I so clearly remember talking to a friend who said, 'I'd love to spend a year travelling.'

I replied, 'Well, why don't you?'

'Well, we couldn't just go away,' she said.

'Couldn't, or wouldn't?' I replied.

If we really do want to do something – if we're not just being wistful – then we have to work out how to do it, or time will pass and we'll never have achieved our dreams. To quote Mahatma Gandhi once again: 'Live as if you were to die tomorrow. Learn as if you were to live forever.'

CHAPTER 22
AND FINALLY ...

It's now ten years since I started *Strictly Come Dancing* – the show that has given me a decade of wonderful experiences – and I wanted to mark this significant year by finally bringing my book to fruition and sharing my inner thoughts with you. I'm so grateful to have been given the opportunity to have my first book published, but let's all remind ourselves that it started with an idea. The idea became a dream. And the dream began to take shape. I began to write the book and wouldn't give up until I had a book deal and, trust me, that was no easy matter. But I kept on believing that one day, when the time was right, it would happen.

And it has.

Dancing with Brendan again

Just before the book deal came through, I was invited by the world-famous choreographer Jason Gilkison, who I'd admired since I was in my teens, to work on season 11 of *Strictly Come Dancing* as the assistant choreographer. This was not something I'd put on my dream board and I'd never imagined in a million years that such an opportunity would come my way. But as usual, I believed that it was all part of fate's plan, so I jumped at the chance of working with Jason and being reunited with what has become a brand, and one that I loved so much. It was the brand that launched my media career and introduced me to the people who I had adored working with.

Being asked reminded me, if I needed reminding, always to leave room in your plans to go with the flow when the opportunity arises. It may be the universe guiding you toward your actual goal.

This role segued perfectly into my schedule. Although it was busy, it wasn't as demanding as a dancer's, so I had time for my corporate and private coaching work, and time, too, to take to the stage as Cinderella's Fairy Godmother in a Christmas pantomime at Bridlington on the Yorkshire coast. I believe that everything comes full circle in life and this was one of those moments for me.

I hadn't spoken much to Brendan since leaving the show. Kevin and I had bumped into him and his lovely wife, Zoe, at the odd event. But fate being fate, on my very first day back on *Strictly*, just as I was off to choreograph one of the group numbers with Jason and his other assistant Patrick, we heard Brendan's dance partner, Natalie Lowe, was injured and he needed a stand-in.

Who was everyone's eyes on? Me, of course! And what did I say? 'Yes. Sure! Why not?'

We danced, chatted and laughed, and it was as if all the time in the world had passed and yet no time had passed at all.

When I got home that evening and told Kevin what had happened, he was so happy for me. 'How wonderful,' he said, 'that just shows that you're healed and in a happy place now. That's just how it should be.'

Brendan and I ended up working together many times throughout the series, and I couldn't help but be proud, so proud, of what we have both achieved in the days since our 'beans on toast' years. It's nice to be able to say, 'Yes, time did heal everything in the end.' We came through the darkness and into the light.

Dream, act, believe, succeed ...

I hope you have enjoyed my story and that I have convinced you that dreams can come true when we take action toward them.

Dream

Throughout the book, I have shown you, or at least tried to show you, how to narrow down what your dreams are, set goals, and how visualizing can help you achieve them. Before I finish my book, I want to share this interesting little story with you from my own experience with the dream board. Remember the dream board? Going into season five, the year I danced with Gethin Jones, I had made a collage of my dreams and goals using pictures and inspirational words. I always tell my clients to put their dream boards where they can see them. Contrary to my own advice I put mine in my wardrobe! There was one more thing I had forgotten to do though. I had not been specific, as I was to find out. A year later, way before I went into my last season of *Strictly*, I found the dream board as I was tidying up. When I had a look at it I realized that I had drawn a trophy on it and written '*Strictly Come Dancing* Champion' above it ... but I hadn't done what I tell everyone else to do – I hadn't been specific! I had forgotten to pinpoint the year and date that I'd win it! I thought to myself that I'd got close coming third with Gethin, but I hadn't been specific enough, so I grabbed a pen and wrote 2008 next to it and threw it back in the wardrobe and actually forgot all about it until some time after I had won. I found it once again after I had left *Strictly*, took a look at it and smiled to myself when I realized that the dream I had put out into the universe had come true.

Act

I am passionate about the fact that if you want something in your life, it is not enough just to set your goals, you have to take action toward achieving them. And that means noticing opportunities when they come your way, and opening your mind to possibilities. For example, how many times in your life has someone given you their business card or number and said, 'Give me a call sometime,' or, 'Stay in touch.' And how many times have you thought, 'I'm sure they say that to everyone.' Well, you must know by now that I believe in connecting with people and that we all have something to share – even if it's just a couple of words or a snippet of information – that can help the people we meet. Otherwise why would our old friend fate have decreed we should meet? For example, about five years ago, when my first fitness DVD came out, I did a cover shoot with *Bodyfit*, a fitness magazine. I had such fun on the shoot and really loved working with the editor and the team. When it was time to say goodbye, the editor gave me her card and said, 'Give me call sometime – I'm not sure how yet, but I would love to work with you again in the future.'

When you decide to embark on a project, don't give up

When I got home, I put the card on my desk where I could see it, my mind, as usual, open for ideas. Now, I have always loved writing and one day an idea for a column popped into my head. I was just thinking about a one-off feature at the time – just some words about fitness and wellbeing, things I passionately wanted to share. I wrote it up and sent it over to the editor who had given me her card, asking if it was of any interest to her. Well, thank goodness I did. Not only did she like it, she liked it so much that she asked if I'd like to write a monthly column. And that's how I got into writing and the world of word counts and deadlines, of having to come up with something to write about every month. I have learned so much through writing my column. That has led to more columns and blogs, and these gave me the confidence to start writing this book (and when I start something I see it through) and I did not give up at the first, second or third hurdle. I was determined to keep going until the right publisher emerged.

My writing journey has taught me several things, but the most important of them was patience. Before I started to write this book, patience was something I had for my clients, but not for myself. I always wanted things done yesterday, but writing the book took time, and all I could do was keep writing and keep trusting that the universe had a plan. And I can't think of a better way to be taught patience.

Believe

Along my journey, every time a doubt came into my head, I read 'Keep Going', the poem on page 82. It never fails to help me turn my doubts around and remind me why I am pursuing a particular dream – whether to become a top professional dancer, to act on stage, or to have my first book published. You know by now that like everyone else, I've had mountains to climb. Things didn't happen overnight. The key to success, and I believe this with all my heart, is that when you decide to embark on a project, don't give up until you're standing on top of the mountain, looking at the wonderful view.

Succeed

At the start of this book, I set you an exercise – now try it again.

Write the word 'success' in the middle of a sheet of paper and draw a circle round it.

Next, draw lines from this centre point, like a spider's legs. Then at the end of each one, write down exactly what comes to your mind when you think about success. It doesn't matter if it's positive or negative. Take a good look at your spider diagram – how much has changed since reading this book? Have your thoughts changed? What are your answers now?

Success means many things to many people but if I have to sum it up in a few words, to me it means feeling happy inside, being able to live in the now, choosing to do things that make me happy and which help contribute to other people's happiness. Success also means achieving something that I find fun and interesting, that I'm passionate about and that I believe in. And it is also about choosing to love, to be kind, and to be surrounded by lovely people with whom we can share our love and laughter.

Follow your dreams. Your happiness is worth it!

CHAPTER 23
MY JOURNEY
CONTINUES: 2013–2019

When I delivered the final manuscript for my third book, *It's Not You, It's Me*, last year (OMG, did I just say third book? That feels surreal …), my publisher told me she had been thinking about re-releasing my first book *Strictly Inspirational* in paperback. She asked me to write a new chapter to bring it up to date and include everything that had happened since it was first published six years ago. I was delighted when she told me it would have a new cover, the one I'd always dreamt of, one that would focus on why I wrote it in the first place – to inspire the reader to know that magical things can happen and dreams come true when we believe they will and take action toward them.

So to add this new chapter, I've reflected back on my now almost six years in LA with my husband. Never in a million years did I know when I moved here, to follow my passion and dream of writing my first book, that I would have three self-help books published in that time, that I would have danced my 2008 *Strictly Come Dancing* winning dance with Tom Chambers 31 times, that meditation would become such a big part of my life and my coaching business, and that I would become the head judge on *Dancing with the Stars* in New Zealand, seated on the judging panel next to my client Julian, who I mentioned in

Chapter 21. In my personal life, I didn't know that my husband would have reinvented his entire career, that our beloved dog Sven would be chasing baseballs in heaven by now, and that my dear Far would have joined him too. So, although there have been so many magical moments over the last six years, I have also had to face the grief of losing my Far and Sven. And although certain life events, like getting married or having children, can make you feel like a grown-up, I felt that losing my Far kicked me right into the proper adult club.

I have talked about grief in this book already, so I won't dwell on it in this new chapter (I think I could probably fill a whole book with what I have learnt and am still learning), but I wanted to share how immensely grateful I have been for the practice of meditation throughout this difficult time, both as I sat with my Far at the end of his life and after his passing. Meditation supports me daily, and if you are struggling with something similar and need a supporting voice to guide you, I would urge you to try it. (I've included some meditations that you can listen to online in the resources section, including some of my own recordings.)

As I'm typing this, and in all those moments when I feel like curling up in a ball and crying my eyes out because I miss my Far so much in the physical world, I take inspiration from some of the last words he said to me: 'I need you to keep walking and never look back.' This powerful statement injects forward motion for me every time I think of it. And, well, as for our beloved dog Sven – his memory is very much alive, as my husband and I talk about him most days. I'm grateful for the wonderful memories and the fact that I have my spiritual practice. I believe in energy and that it never goes just because someone is not physically here. As Marianne Williamson said, 'What has been created by love can never be uncreated.'

My Far also showed me the power of gratitude. Even as he suffered and was in terrible pain from the cancer at the end, he practised gratitude until his last breath. I have a gratitude practice I use all the time to change my mood, and if you haven't already made being thankful part of your life then I urge you to do so. Science even shows that gratitude works to improve our mental health.

TRY THIS ...

Make it your morning practice to simply list as many things as you can that you feel grateful for in the first three minutes of waking up. Notice what feelings are flowing through you as you do this.

Nobody fails in Hollywood, some just leave too early

I want to be clear about our move to LA and starting over in a new country. It was by no means a smooth ride without challenges – it's just that Kevin and I decided that we were going to make LA our home and that, whatever happened, we would be fully committed to making it work. That meant we rolled up our sleeves and worked hard. For the first three years, I had to travel back to the UK a lot. I was scaling down my business and dancing gigs in the UK to afford to invest in my coaching business in LA.

Soon after we arrived, I remember someone saying it can take three to five years to be successful here and that nobody fails in 'Hollywood' – some people just leave too early. I think part of that is true, and it was three years before I could say I had completely moved my business to LA and made enough connections to create a network and possibilities for myself in the States. I have seen many magical reinventions, including my own and Kevin's, where people move to LA with one career in mind but, once there, intuition guides them in a different direction. These are people who have stayed open to the possibility that there was a different path meant for them and have followed it, ending up with a career and life they enjoy.

I'll never forget the day Kevin told me over dinner that he wasn't sure he wanted to be an actor any longer. I felt the fear set in immediately and there was a bit of 'Are you kidding me? You are finally in Hollywood and you have years of experience and now you tell me this.' I feared that the two of us reinventing ourselves at the same time was going to affect us financially and realized we would both have to make some adjustments while we found our stride. However, it meant the second book I was writing at the time, *Reinvent ME*, had even more purpose. It was written for exactly these times – when we feel stuck and lost, whether in relationships or in our careers, and are facing upheaval but have no idea what the future will look like. It was not ideal for Kevin and me to be going through this at similar times, but I knew it was necessary if we were to truly live a life that was aligned with our soul purpose on this planet.

Unplug meditation

As meditation became a daily practice for me, I felt more in tune with my intuition, and one of my friends from the UK, who had also moved to LA, told me about a studio called Unplug Meditation that she thought I would love. Unplug Meditation was the first of its kind in the world – it was like a dry bar for meditation, with different types of classes all day long, including aromatherapy, guided meditation and sound baths. I immediately headed down there to take a class and to write about it for my column in a UK magazine, *Health and Wellbeing*. As soon as I walked through the doors, I felt as if I had come home. I took the class and then went straight to the owner of the studio, Suze Yalof Schwartz, and told her that I didn't want to leave – that I felt like I was meant to coach and teach meditation and hypnosis there. Suze, who is now a dear friend, told me that there were many people who wanted to teach there. I went home that evening and told Kevin how strongly I felt that I needed to be there. I kept going back to meditate at Unplug and about a month later Suze asked me to audition. I had been teaching and recording meditations for years for my clients, but I had never taught meditation in a larger group setting – only hypnosis – so I was a little nervous at first. However, Suze hired me and even passed the last class she was teaching to me, which was a huge honour.

Since that day I have done, and still do, many collaborations with Suze and Unplug. I even convinced Suze to add special group hypnosis classes to the schedule, which I love to teach. This story once again confirms what I spoke about earlier: when I sent in that one short article to the magazine editor, which became a magazine column that I still write to this day and in turn inspired me to write books. In this case it all started with walking into Unplug Meditation, writing about it, and then it becoming such a huge part of my life.

Representing Unplug has taken me to New York, San Francisco and Portugal, to mention just a few places, and I have hosted corporate meditations for them all over the States and met some wonderful clients, as well as recording many meditations for the Unplug app. I'm thankful I have learnt to trust my intuition and that gut feeling and have felt able to communicate when I feel something is aligned.

One thing I've really learnt from living in LA is that if you don't let people know what you feel drawn to, and would like to do, they can't possibly help you. I probably wouldn't be working with Unplug if I hadn't told Suze how I felt, which is hard to believe now because I appreciate our community so much, both as a teacher and as a student, and being part of this studio has pushed me to continually learn and add new skills. Since I started there I have added crystal sound and reiki healing to my skillset. I hope this little story from my life will inspire and remind you how taking just one action toward something you find interesting can put you in a situation that is absolutely where you are meant to be, and bring you closer to your dreams, goals and soul purpose.

Strictly Come Dancing tour 2015

By now you know how much I love a dream board, right? Remember my story in Chapter 22, about the dream board I made with the *Strictly Come Dancing* glitter ball on it – how I wasn't specific on it at first and then added 2008 onto it, which was the year that I won it with Tom. Well, when I left the show in 2008 I created another dream board, visualizing my dream of becoming a judge on the show. I even went to the trouble of cutting out the photos of the judging desk and adding my face onto the line-up next to the other judges. I ended up going for an interview, when a position became available, but the job went to someone else. Years later, in 2014, when I got offered the job to judge on the tour with Craig Revel Horwood and Tom, I went back to my vision board to check it and discovered that the pictures I had used of the judges and the desk were from the *Strictly Come Dancing* tour magazine, rather than the actual TV show. So it had worked, I guess, but if I wanted to be on the show I should have used the pictures from the show. The lesson here *again* is BE SPECIFIC!

The tour was so much fun, though. When I choreographed the winning 2008 dance, I'd thrown everything but the kitchen sink into it, thinking it was only going to be danced once on the night of the final, not 31 shows in a row! It was so magical to perform it live in front of such huge, supportive audiences and to get a chance to thank some of the people who had voted for us and helped win the glitter ball. It was also really special to dance it live in front of my parents, as they hadn't been there on the night of the final.

Little did I know, as I sat there at the desk with Tom and Craig, that it would also be my preparation for becoming the head judge on *Dancing with the Stars* in New Zealand. Now remember Julian who I mentioned in Chapter 21, who I had promised we would move to LA? Well I have been his life coach for quite some years and he gave me permission to share with you that while helping him manifest the job as a judge in New Zealand on *Dancing with the Stars*, I also somehow manifested me sitting next to him as the head judge. Although I really wanted to stay with the *Strictly* family in the UK, it meant so much to be invited to join the New Zealand team. As you know, Brendan and I had been New Zealand champions and we had owned a house there and had hoped to one day call it home. I hadn't been back since we split up and I missed it so much. I was so grateful for the opportunity to go back to this magical place – I literally cried the minute I stepped foot on New Zealand soil. It's hard to do justice to this sacred land with words, as its beauty has to be felt. I felt this was very much my dancing life coming full circle, but it was my goal to go there and give constructive feedback using the skills from my life coaching business, and to use this new platform to spread the word about meditation and how powerful it can be in supporting our mental health.

As my coaching business and network grew in the States, it became apparent to me that I had to commit to my US dream 100 per cent of the time, which meant I had to start saying no to gigs that kept taking me back to the UK, including yearly pantomimes and dancing with Ian. It was clear to me where my passion lay – in my writing, life coaching and speaking business. In 2017 I retired officially from my professional dance career with one last dance tour. The last night Ian and I danced, on a beautiful full moon night by the ocean, felt

To truly flow in life, we must be willing to let go of things to create space for new opportunities.

so right – I knew I was ready to let that part of my life and career go, and I haven't looked back since. These days writing, life coaching, hypnosis and meditation fill my days, and my heart has never been more full, but I will be forever grateful for everything dance and living life as an athlete taught me – I often draw on the experiences in my work. To truly flow in life, we must be willing to let go of things to create space for new opportunities. You cannot add to an already overcrowded wardrobe in your house or in your life.

Our new bundle of joy

I know, reading this heading, you probably instantly thought 'Aww bless, they've had a baby,' so bear with me! About three years ago we rescued another young dog called Charlie and she became Sven's best friend. We had visualized a little doggie who loved cuddles. One evening Kevin went online to look at dogs who needed a home and up popped a photo of Charlie. We drove to the rescue home and as soon as I held her in my arms I could feel that she was a bundle of pure love, and the rest is history. Sounds romantic? Well I didn't mention she pooped whilst I was holding her – less glamorous now, right? I took it as a sign, though, that she was relaxed in my company. She immediately wanted to be Sven's best friend and Sven didn't seem to mind. They quickly fell asleep next to each other and she was by Sven's side every day until his last breath. She has been such a joy for us through the loss too. A real bundle of love.

The pressures of social media

When I first wrote this book, I had just moved to LA and opened an Instagram account. I had used Twitter before but had not really got the handle of Instagram, and I was turned down for certain opportunities because of my lack of followers. What I see a lot from my clients, and sometimes for myself too, is that on days when we are not feeling our best, the need to compare our journey to others online can arise. So many times people have told me they need to have a bigger following to do 'xyz', but luckily I didn't let that stop me. It kind of reminded me of back in the day when certain dance coaches used to think they knew what I was capable of and were busy telling me I wouldn't make it and that I should just give up. I learnt back then that action speaks louder than words and I simply focused on my journey and my goals and kept myself accountable, taking action each day toward my dreams.

Please know that although social media is a great way of sharing and connecting, there are so many ways to do business, and the most important thing is to follow what feels authentic to you and the rest will follow. If I had accepted the publishers who told me I didn't have a big enough following to write and sell a book, then I would not be sitting typing this today. I reframed that feedback to *they* were not the right publishers for me and I kept searching until I found the right fit for me. They say when we know, we know, so if you feel inspired to do something with every fibre of your body and your intuition is guiding you, I would lean in hard and follow your own inner compass.

If you feel inspired to do something with every fibre of your body and your intuition is guiding you, I would lean in hard and follow your own inner compass.

Anything is possible

As I finish this chapter, I want to leave you with this thought – sometimes the difference between making it happen and not making it happen (achieving something and not achieving something) is just the difference between actually doing it and simply not doing it, or believing it will happen or believing it won't. All I needed to get my first book deal was to believe in myself and that I could do it. And what was vital to remember was *why* I was doing it. I wanted to write for the same reason I wanted to become a life coach, to be of service in this world and to pass on the tools I knew were helpful and could support others. My dream of being an author was not about the money but rather from a desire to have an outlet through which I could serve on a bigger scale and help people. I was seeking a team who I could learn from in the publishing field, as this was all new to me – someone who believed in me and what I was trying to achieve through this book. We often think we need many people, but in fact having just one person who believes in us and understands our vision is enough, and having that one publisher, Jo, who took a bet on me, was the beginning of a whole new chapter in my life (pun intended) and here we are. I hope you know by now that it wasn't that I had more luck and magic than anyone else to make my dreams a reality. I simply dreamt of it, visualized it, made a plan and then action by action and hard work I did it. Just the way you can too.

- Do you have a dream?
- Are you ready to believe in yourself?
- Are you ready to do what it takes to make it a reality?
- If yes, start now and make a plan of action.

There is always one small thing we can do right now, even if it's just doing some research or reading a helpful book that will support our dream. You got this. I believe in you! Remember, everyone has something unique to share with the world, including you!

SUGGESTED BOOKS

Bernstein, Gabrielle, *Spirit Junkie* and *Miracles Now*, Hay House
This author has a funky young way about her, which is very engaging. *Spirit Junkie* is a great introduction into motivational self-help books. She also teaches about a course in miracles from her perspective. I became aware and now practice kundalini yoga thanks to her recommendation.

Branson, Richard, *Losing My Virginity*, Virgin Publishing
Read this a long time ago. My favourite part of the book is where Richard talks about starting out and how he never lost his self-belief. He never gave up – even when all the banks said no, he knew one would say yes.

Brown, Brené, *The Gifts of Imperfection*, Hazelden
So helpful to be reminded of how we should be kind to ourselves.

Byrne, Rhonda, *The Magic* and *The Secret*, Atria Books
What I love about these books is that they sum up so many great ideas in a very straightforward way.

Chopra, Deepak, *The Healing Self*, Rider
This book really nudges you into looking at healing in a new way and to deeper understand the mind body connection. Fantastic book I will return to again and again.

Ferriss, Timothy, *The 4-Hour Work Week*, Vermilion
This is what I call 'how to work smart'. I love this book, and it helped me hugely in my time management.

Hay, Louise, *You Can Heal Your Life*, Hay House
My 'go-to' book – I love the affirmations and suggestions she gives. Her life story is fascinating, and Louise is a huge inspiration to me. It describes how different emotions can be linked to different diseases. This book comes with me whenever I travel.

Massey, Alexandra, *Beat Depression Fast*, Watkins
I love this story because the author describes so honestly how she found her way out of a depression – not by using drugs, but by self-discovery and using the exercises described in this wonderful book.

McGee, Paul, *S.U.M.O. (Shut up, Move on)*, Capstone
Different approach, with good exercises for work or home life.

McKenna, Paul, *Instant Confidence*, Bantam Press
This was my go-to book, mostly on repeat, when I was feeling low.

O'Connor, Joseph, *NLP Workbook*, HarperCollins
This book helped me greatly when I was studying NLP.

Pueblo, Yung, *Inward*, Andrews McMeel Publishing
I have never met anyone like Yung Pueblo who is able to describe huge life lessons in such few and precise words to get powerful messages across on every page. I was honored when he agreed to write the foreword for my third book *It's Not You, It's Me*.

Redfield, James, *The Celestine Prophecy*, Bantam Press
This book was vital in my career. It has taught me to stay openminded when I meet new people, and not be afraid to ask, talk and share information.

Robbins, Anthony, *Awaken the Giant Within*, Simon & Schuster
This was an empowering read when I needed it most. Anthony Robbins always speaks with such authority – I find that engaging in itself.

Spackman, Dr Kerry, *The Winner's Bible*, HarperCollins
I love this – everyone should create a winner's bible for themselves.

Tolle, Eckhart, *The Power of Now*, New World Library and *A New Earth*, Penguin
These were such wonderful books. I refer to them often when I get pulled off track and want reminding of how to live in the now.

Virtue, Doreen, *Chakra Clearing* (audio), Hay House
I love this audio, especially if I have been surrounded by lots of people or negativity. It helps me feel centred and cleansed.

Virtue, Doreen, *The Lightworker's Way*, Hay House
Beautiful story about how Doreen started out.

Williamson, Marianne, *A Course in Miracles*, Foundation for Inner Peace
I recommend doing the exercises in this book if you are going through a tough time, and are searching for a deep spiritual text to find self-love.

Williamson, Marianne, *A Return to Love*, HarperCollins
To me Marianne is the queen bee of inspirational speakers. I go to listen to her live as much as possible when I'm in LA. She teaches the principles of *A Course in Miracles*, which is quite a heavy text to read, which is I why I love this book – it describes the principles in an more accessible way.

WATKINS

Sharing Wisdom Since 1893

The story of Watkins Publishing dates back to March 1893, when John M. Watkins, a scholar of esotericism, overheard his friend and teacher Madame Blavatsky lamenting the fact that there was nowhere in London to buy books on mysticism, occultism or metaphysics. At that moment Watkins was born, soon to become the home of many of the leading lights of spiritual literature, including Carl Jung, Rudolf Steiner, Alice Bailey and Chögyam Trungpa.

Today our passion for vigorous questioning is still resolute. With over 350 titles on our list, Watkins Publishing reflects the development of spiritual thinking and new science over the past 120 years. We remain at the cutting edge, committed to publishing books that change lives.

DISCOVER MORE AT:
www.watkinspublishing.com

Read our blog

Watch and listen to
our authors in action

Sign up to
our mailing list

We celebrate conscious, passionate, wise and happy living.

Be part of that community by visiting

/watkinspublishing   **@watkinswisdom**

/watkinsbooks   @watkinswisdom